MOSAIC ART

DESIGN AND INSPIRATION

MARTIN CHEEK

NEW HOLLAND

Contents

Introduction

THIS IS NOT meant to be a 'how to make mosaics' book and neither is it a sourcebook in the true sense, since nearly all of the work shown was designed by one person – me! It is not intended that you should copy any of the works shown here, but rather that you should be inspired by them and want to make your own, personal mosaics. The collection of my mosaics shown in this book includes much of my recent work, as well as some of the larger pieces I have tackled over the years.

Starting out

I spent many years as a puppet animator and although on the surface this seems to be entirely unrelated to mosaics, it is, in fact, very similar. The thought processes needed for making mosaics are parallel to those needed for animation. Questions such as, 'How many pieces are in that mosaic?' seem totally irrelevant to me. No one would ever think to ask, 'How many bricks are in that wall?' or, 'How many stitches are in that jumper?' The wall or jumper either works or doesn't; it stands up or falls apart.

Similarly, the phrase, 'You must be so patient!' is often thrown at me. The answer is, yes and no. When I'm working on a mosaic I am driven by the desire to see it as a finished piece, to see if I was right when I imagined it working at the design stage. But to see me waiting for a bus is an entirely different matter.

Making mosaics

People who don't make mosaics imagine that it is like doing a jigsaw puzzle, and tell me so. Well it's not. A jigsaw puzzle is a puzzle – it has a pre-determined solution. Whether you are brilliantly fast at completing the puzzle, or painfully slow, so long as you do actually finish it, the result will always be the same. A mosaic, on the other hand, will be different every time.

I am constantly amazed by the variety of styles I see on the mosaic courses I run. Nearly eight hundred people have now attended my courses and I can honestly say that each mosaic produced has been individual and different from the rest, even when they were created by the same person. This is illustrated by the enormous variety of work shown in this book, and all but three of the mosaics were designed by me. This is particularly amazing given that mosaic material itself seems so inflexible at first glance.

Ideas and inspiration

The decision to call this book *Mosaic Art: Design and Inspiration* was no accident. I have included here, for the first time, some of my initial design artwork. These pieces are not meant to be works of art in their own right but working drawings, shown to help demonstrate how I tackle the creative process of making a mosaic. I haven't put in many of my drawings – they were not originally meant for public scrutiny – and they only appear where I thought that their inclusion was relevant to what I was trying to say.

Interestingly, my own sources of inspiration for the works shown in this book range from the Egyptian Pre-Dynastic Naquada I period, 4000-3600BC (Naquada Ram, see p72) and Ancient Greek ware from around 1400BC (Palm Pot, see p124), through to Art Nouveau, 1890-1910 (Owl Jar, see p122) and modern abstract painting (Machynlleth Mela Mural, see p60). So my message is: as well as flipping through trendy magazines, glossy books and colour supplements for your inspiration, go down to your local museum or library and do some research there as well.

Martin Cheek

PART ONE

The elements of design

Creating a design

THE DESIGN IS always the starting point for any mosaic. Even if you simply play with shapes and let your imagination make something out of them, like my Cheeky Fusion Birds on p54, then you can still be said to be designing a piece of work.

If you are struggling to get the relationship right of say, two fish swimming together, it is a good idea to draw them and then tear them out and try different arrangements of the elements. If you work on a sheet of paper then there is a natural tendency to see the edges of your paper as the parameters of your design. By tearing the subjects out you automatically free yourself from this constraint. So the two fish could be swimming up to each other, swimming past each other or completely ignoring each other, depending on where in the design you place them.

I tend to work on a small scale at first, in order to resolve the composition and get the relationships right. When I am happy with this preliminary study I then scale the design up and work on a full-sized version. Using charcoal and coloured pastels is a good way of avoiding getting into tiny fiddly detail, which you will be unable to recreate in mosaic. The thickness of a charcoal stick is about as small as you will be able to manage when cutting the tesserae.

In this section I have tried to explain the design considerations that I consider important in my work. Mosaics, by their very nature take a long time to make, so it is really worth putting in the effort to get the design right. Don't think that a poor design will be all right when mosaiced – in my experience this is rarely the case.

Contrast

A COMMON DIFFICULTY when making a mosaic is achieving enough contrast between the subject and the background. There are many different ways of achieving contrast, so here are some examples that can be easily identified within the covers of this book.

Tonal contrasts

The easiest way to think of tonal contrast is to imagine that the colour image was photocopied in black and white – so two completely different colours, say blue and red, may come out as exactly the same shade of grey. If they did then it would be true to say that they were tonally the same. Where mosaics often fail to work is when the tone of the subject, a fish for example, is the same tone as the background, the sea. When seen from a distance it becomes difficult to distinguish the subject from the background. One solution would be to make the background tonally darker, as in the Fish Panel, below (see also p23).

Another solution is to make the background tonally paler, as in the Wildlife Table, below right (see also p90). The soft pastel shades of vitreous glass, which look so uninspiring when compared to the brighter metal-veined range, are, in fact, extremely useful when choosing a background colour. They will 'push back' the background and allow your subject to stand out. You will find all of this paler range – blue, green, pink, mauve and fawn – used for backgrounds in many of the mosaics in this book.

Warm or cool colour contrasts

Colour contrast is different to tonal contrast. A warm colour – one that contains red – will appear to come forward against a cool colour – one that contains blue. The contrast between red and blue is obvious, but this device can also be applied to two browns: reddish-brown Burnt Sienna can be used to highlight or enhance a cool Brown Umber, as in the Pterodactyl, below centre (see also p34).

Fish Panel (DETAIL)
100x100cm (39x39in), vitreous glass, 2000

The dark grey background of this panel enhances the lighter tones of the sea creatures mosaiced into it.

Pterodactyl (DETAIL)
50cm (19in) diameter, Cinca ceramic, 2000-2001

The subtle colour contrasts in this panel keep it looking strong and clear, while allowing an overall harmony.

Wildlife Table (DETAIL)
335½x152cm (132x60in), vitreous glass, 1998

On this table, the light-coloured background throws the darker animals forward.

Contrasts in tile sizes

Placing larger, un-cut tiles next to the cut quarter-tile tesserae will draw the eye to the more detailed and finer work within the piece. The Underwater Panel, below (see also p84), is a very good example of this contrast technique.

Reflective and non-reflective materials

Shiny, reflective vitreous glass tesserae will always appear to stand proud of the matt, non-reflective Cinca ceramic tesserae. This is particularly useful if you mosaic your subject in glass against a ceramic background – in strong light the subject will leap out of the picture. Unfortunately this effect is difficult to reproduce in a book, as the paper and printing inks are shiny! You can also use mirror tiles to the same effect, as in the Golden Dragon, below.

It is interesting to compare the two hares, bottom left, as they are the same design made up in different mediums: shiny glass and non-reflective ceramic.

Underwater Panel
200cm (78in) diameter, Cinca ceramic, 2000

The large uncut tiles lend a regularity to the background, which highlights the movement created by the cut tiles within the fish.

Golden Dragon
31x31cm (12x12in), Cinca ceramic, Astoria ceramic and gold mirror, 2001

I treat gold mirror as a sort of poor man's gold leaf smalti. It can look similar to the gold leaf in a certain light; the main difference is that as it is mirror with a gold silvering, it gives off a golden reflection, which I like a lot.

There is no point in trying to compete with all that gold, so the simple terracotta back-ground, which gives good tonal contrast, as well as letting the gold shine out, seemed to me to be a good choice.

Sitting Hare
58x31cm (22x12in), (RIGHT) vitreous glass, 1998
(FAR RIGHT) Cinca ceramic, 2000

There is something very magical and mystical about the hare. I tried to capture that quizzical but knowing look here. The strip of white on his underside isn't much

but it's very important, especially the way that it continues behind the foreleg and along the tail. Lines that link up visually act as construction lines and give the mosaic a unity.

(FAR RIGHT) Here is the same design mosaiced in Cinca ceramic. This hare looks calmer, friendlier and all together less wild. This mosaic benefits greatly from the spectrum of browns, which is excellent in this particular range of tiles.

Chicken and Egg
28x35cm (11x13in), vitreous glass and sculpted stoneware pieces, 2000

The only true mosaic in this piece is the sky and the grass, the chicken and egg being chunky pieces of *opus sectile*. The shiny vitreous glass tesserae surrounding the subtly glazed ceramic pieces provide another illustration of how a mix of reflective and non-reflective materials can add another dimension to a mosaic.

Contrasts in thickness

Different levels within a mosaic also give contrast. Placing a 6mm- (¼in-) thick tile alongside 3mm- (⅛in-) thick glass or ceramic tesserae will make the tile stand proud. While this is not practical if you want a flat tabletop, this method of including larger tiles, or ceramic pieces known as *opus sectile*, is a great way of achieving contrast on wall panels or murals, as in Cheeky Bird, below.

A flat mosaic is obviously easier to clean than a bumpy one – you just rub a damp cloth over it. However, I think too much emphasis is put on whether a mosaic is flat or not and unless it's for a table or a floor, I always prefer to see a mosaic with varying thicknesses.

Contrasts in texture

This is a great way to add contrast and make your mosaics even more tactile, though it is only appropriate when the finished mosaic doesn't need to be flat.

Because I have a pottery with a kiln, I am able to sculpt *opus sectile* in clay and raku fire or glaze them. Making your own elements in this way is great fun, especially when you cast them and swap them with other mosaicists. Sculpt the object out of clay or modelling material onto a flat surface – glass or a smooth kitchen worktop is perfect. Make a simple mould from wood or card around the sculpted piece and pour plaster of Paris into it. Leave the plaster to dry for a few days in a warm place before using the mould. If you don't have access to a kiln, then there are lots of 'cold cure' materials on the market, as well as modelling materials that you can bake hard in a domestic oven. Of course, you don't have to make a mould, but I find it worth it, as you can then reproduce the elements as many times as you want. Soon you will build up a collection of moulds that will come in useful in the future.

Another way to add texture is to include found objects in your mosaics. Start collecting ceramics from junk shops and charity shops. It doesn't even matter if the pieces are broken, in fact it is a bonus if they are, as it reduces the

Cheeky Bird
32x32cm (13x13in), vitreous glass and raku-fired pieces, 2000

This piece was made on my summer mosaics course in Greece. For the *opus sectile* elements of this bird, templates were drawn and the pieces carved accurately to match them. Shelby, one of the students, cast the roundel in the top right-hand corner. We all made motifs such as this, moulded and slip-cast them and then traded them with each other to use in our mosaics.

I like to respond to whatever is around me, this acts as reminder of the trip and the piece itself becomes a souvenir. A good example are the top and bottom borders on this panel, which were taken from a child's entrance ticket to the museums of Greece.

price. Look for beads, buttons, shells and pebbles that can be incorporated into a mosaic. For example, I used an 'evil eye' in the Greeky Bird on p49, a piece of beach flint for the eye of the Naquada Ram on p72 and beach glass on the water of the Leaping Frog on p119.

While found objects don't give you the control you have when making your own elements, they can offer some interesting results. After a while you will train your eye to spot objects – unusual bottle tops, cosmetic accessories, faux jewels, florist's glass pebbles – that will look good in your mosaics. The more things you have to choose from the better, and I find that playing with various materials is very much part of the creative process. Sometimes they are even the original inspiration behind the piece.

Contrasts in shape

This is another useful device for bringing vitality to a mosaic. You can cut tiles into quite specific shapes and lay them among regular tiles. Any mosaic will usually include

at least two types of contrast: I made 'Any Eggs?', below, to demonstrate how one mosaic can include all of them.

Detail (FOLLOWING PAGES)

Capturing the character of my subject is vital to me. The eyes are often the single most important feature in this – get the eyes wrong and you'll never achieve the desired result. Equally, if the characterisation is falling short, it's probably because the eyes aren't quite right. Lining the eyes up, so that they are both focused on the same thing, is essential, unless you want the dazed expression that occurs when they aren't! The eyes on the following pages are made from fusions and tesserae and show how different materials and shapes can capture different expressions.

The Garfish's eye on p32 could not now be mistaken for anything other than an eye. However, when I chose it, it was just another piece in my box of fusions. It's not unusual for me to try several examples and keep them in place for a few days before deciding which one looks best.

'Any Eggs?'
31x59cm (12x23in), vitreous glass and Cinca ceramic, 1999

Placing 'splintered' shapes of tesserae next to the usual square ones will clearly differentiate the soft roundness of the chicken from the spiky straw. I like the way that the straw radiates out from the bird, emphasising the fact that she is firmly roosted in her bed.
  I keep chickens and the startled look of surprise if you disturb one while she is roosting on an egg seemed to me to be worth capturing. Mine cluck disdainfully as if to say, 'How can a girl get any peace around here?' – and yes, she is supposed to look like a chicken drumstick.

Pierrot, Pulcinella and Harlequin
128x95cm
(50½x37½in),
vitreous glass, 1993

The spiralling and radiating lines of the background are given added emphasis by the random darker tesserae that cluster more thickly where the sweeping lines collide.

Colour

FOR SOME ARTISTS, colour and texture could be said to be a main driving force. Cleo Mussi and Kaffe Fassett both spring to mind: they are both textile artists who now make mosaics and their mosaics exude a wonderful sense of colour and pattern that makes their work unique. Personally, I tend to think of mosaic as a medium, as the means of expression – the language if you like – and not the thing in itself. I could use a different medium, water-colour for example, and often do so. It's a case of choosing the best route for what you are trying to say.

Quantity of colour

It's interesting to note that the amount of any given colour you use doesn't necessarily mean that that colour will stand out the most. In the mosaic Pierrot, Pulcinella & Harlequin, left, the quantity of gold tesserae used numbers the least as a percentage of the whole mosaic, but stands out the most! In the 'peppering' of the background the mauves and purples shine out from the soft pink, although there is eight times as much pink used as mauves or purples. Why is this? Simply because of the tonal contrast of these chosen colours.

As usual, I had to see if I could stretch this point to its ultimate conclusion. In the mosaic of a Herring Gull, below (see also p27), I used only one single piece of red smalti to denote the spot on its beak, and it sings promi-nently out of the whole mosaic.

Herring Gull
32x39cm (12x15in), vitreous glass, gold mirror & smalti, 2001

In nature, the red spot on the beak is meant to stand out, as it forms a target for the chicks to aim at when feeding.

Range of colour

It goes without saying that the choice of colours is one of the most important aspects in any mosaic. If you are using marble or natural stone or pebbles, then the choice is obviously going to be limited to what is available in the natural environment around you. The Naquada Ram, below (see also p72), is, I think, a particularly successful example of what can be achieved with natural materials.

I actually enjoy the restrictions imposed upon the design when faced with a limited palette. Unlike paints you can't 'mix' mosaic colours – you have to achieve the effect of 'mixing' by placing the different colours next to each other. In terms of painting it's like the pointillism achieved by Seurat. When viewed from a distance the brain fuses the individual coloured tesserae together and perceives an overall blanket colour comprising those elements, very much in the way that pixels on a television screen work.

Cinca ceramic has a range of only 25 colours, but this restricted palette often leads to a harmony of colour that simply may not have occurred if one had had access to an unlimited palette.

The vitreous glass Bisazza range has 56 colours, which sounds a lot, but because this material is mainly used for swimming pools, 16 of them are whites, blues and greens (not many people want a bright red swimming pool!). It is really worth having a 25kg (55lb) box of 'loose mix' of these tiles. This mix is in fact the scrap bits and pieces, but because the colours can, and do, vary from batch to batch,

Naquada Ram
41x38cm (16x15in), sand and cement slab, marble, flint eye, 2001

The natural tones of the marble work well in describing the varied, muted colours of the ram's fleece, as the detail on the right shows.

you will often find slightly different shades of the same colour among the scrap.

In the case of smalti, Italian makers Orsoni have a basic range of 100 colours readily available, but they can also match any colour you ask them to. They say that they can offer a total of 5000 colours.

Aids to design

I AM OFTEN asked if I design my mosaics on a computer. The answer is a definite no. It's not that I have anything against the computer, but it's simply not the way I've been trained and I don't think it suits my style. I have to say that most of the mosaics I have seen that have been computer-designed are easy to spot; to me they look stiff and lifeless.

The photocopier is a great tool, I often use one for enlarging my own mosaic designs. Laser copiers are also capable of printing a reverse image, which is an enormous help if you are working indirect, as you can simply follow the printed image rather than having to work out where each of the tesserae go.

I suppose the time will come when we will all use computers to design with; some graphic design art courses already rely on them entirely. But then again, many artists are still driven to paint with oils on canvas. After many thousands of years of this practice, there must be something about the immediacy and sensuality of directly applying paint to canvas with a brush that continues to inspire artists all over the world.

Translating drawn lines
For me there is a creative freedom experienced by drawing directly with a pencil. I draw from the wrist, the elbow or the shoulder, depending on the size of the drawing. When the artworks are translated into mosaics, the fluidity of the lines also comes through, as the details on the right show.

The design process

THE WHOLE PROCESS of developing a mosaic from an initial idea to a finished piece is both fascinating and sometimes frustrating, and you go through it, to some degree or another, with every piece of work. I am fond of the Pompeii mosaics (now in the Archaeological Museum, Naples), as is the client who commissioned this Fish Panel. While neither of us wanted to produce a direct copy, we both felt that homage would be wonderful. This is how this mosaic evolved.

The first stage of any commission is to make some rough sketches showing different compositions. In this case only two variations were required, because the client knew what she had in mind and had already seen something similar in my portfolio.

Having chosen the composition, I then made a full-size design. These days I work on craft paper taken from a huge roll measuring about 90cm (35in) in width. Although it is an expensive outlay, a roll like this will last me about five years. If the design is large then I draw with charcoal, which prevents me making the details too fine to be rendered into mosaic tesserae. Charcoal also has the benefit of being very quick, and you can erase a line with a sweep of your thumb and make a stronger mark over the top. Once this drawing is right, I start work on the mosaic itself.

Fish Panel Final Artwork
100x100cm (39x39in), charcoal and pastel on craft paper, 2000

When I translate the roughs into a full-size artwork, often I draw each character separately and then cut them out and arrange them on a separate sheet to play around with the shapes and the gaps between them. You know when it looks right; you find yourself fiddling and not moving the design any further forward. This is the point at which you must say, 'That's it!' and leave it alone. I find this a very exciting stage, as now I can try to imagine what the finished mosaic will look like.

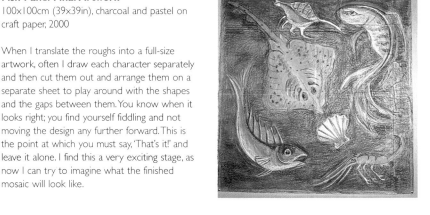

Fish Panel Roughs
Pencil and watercolour on watercolour paper, 2000

The pencil drawings show how the background could be handled *opus regulatum* (top), or *opus musivum* (bottom). We decided that opus musivum was a bit too complicated and that the opus regulatum was preferable in this case, as it would calm down an already quite busy composition.

Fish Panel In Situ
When the Fish Panel was finally installed in the client's bathroom I went to photograph it. However, it was hung in such a way that I actually had to photograph its reflection in the large mirror to get the best angle.

Shrimp
53×36cm (21×14in), smalti, vitreous glass, 2000

My client wasn't sure what medium she wanted for her mosaic. I pressed for smalti because I thought that the fish would benefit from having a larger and subtler range of colours. In order to win her over I made this shrimp, so that she could see how the entire mosaic would look with the subjects rendered in smalti. However, my client didn't like this piece and opted for all vitreous glass instead.

Fish Panel
100×100cm (39×39in), vitreous glass, 2000

My client chose the dark grey background, in keeping with the Pompeii feel. I would have opted for a dark blue or dark viridian, but have to concede that this charcoal colour does give the panel a definite stylish quality. I particularly like the lines of movement of the fish: the 'S' of the dogfish juxtaposed with the diagonal sweep of the ray.

PART TWO

Sources of inspiration

Finding personal inspiration

'WHERE DO YOU get your ideas from?' is a question I am often asked. In this part of the book I will try to answer this seemingly simple, but in fact complex, question.

Inspiration is such a personal thing. We all know that one person's idea of taste is another person's horror. For example, my friend and fellow mosaic artist, Oliver Budd, loves industrial machinery and captures it brilliantly in his mosaic work, whereas I can't tell one engine, aeroplane or car from another. I know that a fire engine is red and an ambulance is white, but that's about it – I'm simply not interested in them. Now birds and animals on the other hand...

What I'm talking about is one's individual visual stimulus – seeing something and being so bowled over by it that you want to try and capture it yourself in mosaic. The sources of inspiration listed on the following pages all work for me, but you need to find your own. Discovering what you are inspired by is like finding out what music you like listening to or what type of food you like to eat; you won't know until you try it.

For example, a trip to the local flea market always works for me. How could the sight of all of those brightly coloured stalls laden with chinaware, carpets and fabrics fail to stimulate the eye?

The decorative arts are also a great source of inspiration to me, whether on buildings, or in collections, museums or shops. Sometimes boldly exuberant, at other times subtly intricate, these objects can be a starting point for your own personal statement.

I know it's an obvious thing to say, but travel is another good way of seeing and experiencing the unexpected. I find that when I'm abroad my senses are heightened. Although it's perfectly feasible that one can return to foreign parts, it always feels as though you're experiencing something special and fleeting that can never be recaptured.

The natural world

THERE IS AN old cliché, which says, 'Write about what you know.' Like most clichés it has an element of truth, and the same can be said for artists. My background is animation so I naturally come to my mosaic work with an animator's eye. What excites me about making a mosaic is trying to capture the character of the creature I'm portraying. I'm interested in that particular herring gull, not just any old herring gull.

Food is also a part of nature and in recent years we have all become more fascinated by what we eat. Aesthetic pleasure is very much a part of this enjoyment and I'm sure that we've all savoured the sight of the luscious, watery-pink flesh of a watermelon, so perfectly balanced by the rich, stripy-greens of the skin. If you cut a red onion or cabbage in half horizontally, you can see many subtle shades of the same colour purple, a visually stimulating palette contained in one neat package.

Markets, especially on a hot summer's day in countries like France and Italy, can provide a stunning spectacle. It's not often that one can see so many different natural shapes and colours in such a small space.

Herring Gull
32x39cm (12x15in), vitreous glass, gold mirror and smalti, 2001

I find the natural world a source of endless fascination and a starting point for many projects. Questions such as, 'Why does the herring gull need that red goneal spot on its lower mandible?' intrigue me into research, which in turn inspires a new mosaic.

Zoos and bird parks

THESE CAN BE rather like museums: if you try to see everything you'll come away with nothing. I try to have a plan in mind as to which animals or birds I want to study that day. To do this you obviously need to have prior knowledge of the collection, so your first visit will, by necessity, be an overview of all the animals. Even if, like me, you don't want the study to be exact in terms of realism, you will still benefit from looking at the animal or bird in detail. Your characterisation might be drawn from a quirky mannerism or a distinctive behaviour trait in that particular animal. Picasso felt that his goat, made out of, among other things, a wicker basket and gourds for the udders, looked more like a goat than a real one. I know what he meant.

Owls are among my favourite birds, as they are so full of character. I was once looking at some very sleepy owls when one of them opened one eye, turned around and looked at me. It made me feel as though I had disturbed it and I later tried to capture that feeling in mosaic.

Cheeky Owl
31x31cm (12x12in), vitreous glass, 2000

I usually spend a month or so every year teaching in Greece, where owls are so prevalent that the Greeks have an old phrase, 'It's like taking owls to Athens.' In other words, don't bother because they've got enough already! Like the Cheeky Bird shown on p50, this bird consists of three basic lines, which can be subtly altered to completely change the character of the owl. The way that these small changes make such a huge difference is what interests me and makes me return to this inquisitive bird.

Inspired by colour

As well as food itself, food packaging can also be bright, colourful and imaginative. I've always admired these designs on their way to the rubbish bin, but lately I've started to save some of them, partly because I've noticed that they change so often these days. I am particularly fond of a paper wrapping from a tin of Italian 'Sardine Piccanti'.

Occasionally one comes across silk-screen printed plastic bags, in greengrocers for example. I particularly love these, especially when the registration has slipped very slightly and the primitive, hands-on printing process becomes apparent.

Sometimes the colour of the actual mosaic material can inspire me and go on to become the starting point for a piece of mosaic art: for example the red tiles in the Cheeky Parrot, below left. At other times it is a range of dazzling colours that starts the mind working, which was the case with the jewel-like fusions that inspired the Fusion Fish, below (see also p52).

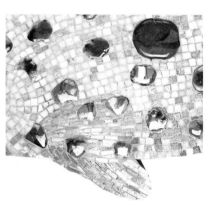

Fusion Fish
78x40cm (30x15in), vitreous glass, raku fired ceramic eye and glass fusions, 2000

This piece was made up from a collection of fusions that I had made, without having any particular home in mind for them at the time.

Cheeky Parrot
30x30cm (12x12in), vitreous glass, 1999

The bright red always reminds me of a parrot whenever I use it, so it was a very natural and obvious choice to use it in a mosaic of a parrot. It just goes to show that inspiration comes from all sources, not least the pure colour of the mosaic tiles themselves.

Humour

MANY OF THE pieces in this book are meant to be witty and the humour in a piece is what motivates me a lot of the time. It is a desire to make the viewer smile when they see it and hopefully recognise what it was that made me smile in the first place.

This doesn't mean that I'm not a serious artist or that I don't take my work seriously – I am and I do. The truth is that it's possible to be serious and be funny.

When my work is humorous, it's usually because it is trying to illustrate a funny aspect of a creature: the length of a garfish, or all ten of the swirly legs of a squid vying for space within the mosaic.

The fusions I used in the birds on these two pages reminded me of the 'eyes' that male peacocks have in their tail feathers. I thought that it would be even more flamboyant to put similar 'eyes' into the hair of these wacky birds of paradise.

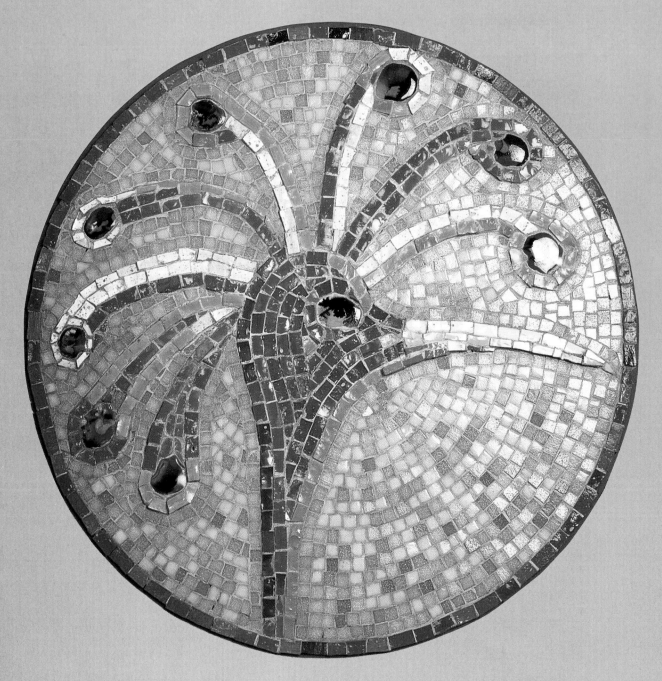

Fusion Birds I and II
50cm (19in) diameter, vitreous glass and glass
fusions, 2000

For the bird on the opposite page, it was
essential that a fusion should be used as his eye,
but achieving this was the trickiest part – I
wanted the bird to look ridiculous, but not
realize it himself and all the eyes that I made
seemed to make him look too serious. This one
is the best that I could manage.

The bird on this page is really a companion
piece to the one opposite. One fusion looked
like a droplet that needed to be hung from a
branch, so I made more to create this
Christmas-tree bird, complete with baubles.

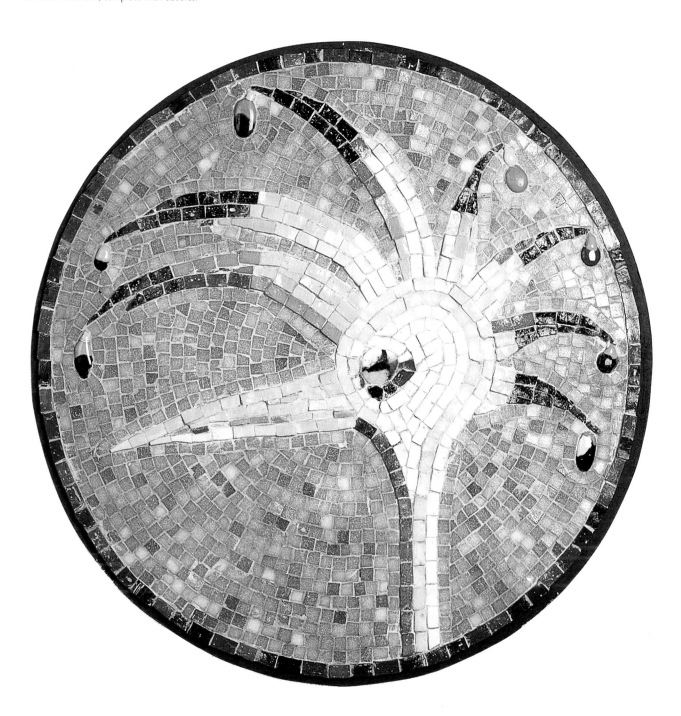

Books

OVER THE YEARS I have built up a large library. I treat my books as tools and have no compunction about writing notes in the margins or, in the case of my nature books, drawing in them. I never feel guilty about buying books, but usually still try to justify the purchase by saying to myself that I will be able to use it to help me make a new piece of work.

If you see a book you think you want in a second-hand or remainder bookshop, my advice is to buy it there and then, as you may not see it again. I'm sure we have all once regretted not buying that once-in-a-lifetime find.

I'm often amazed by the fact that no matter how obscure the subject, someone, somewhere has written a book on it. If I need a boost of inspiration, I often find that a trip to my local second-hand bookshop will do the trick. Let the owner of your bookshop know what you are interested in; he may look out for books for you, as mine does.

Illustrated books on nature are particularly useful to me in my work. Animals and birds have a habit of blending

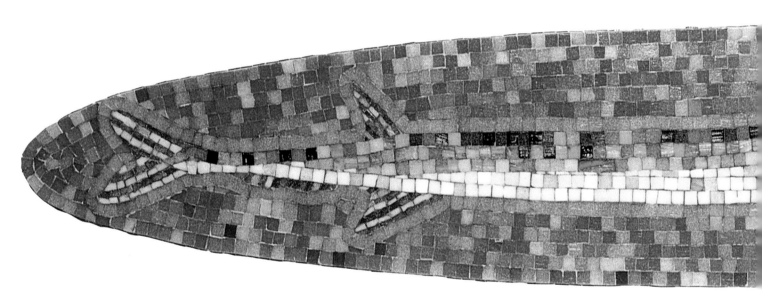

Garfish
124x20cm (48x8in), vitreous glass and glass fusion, 2000

Here is one example of a mosaic inspired by a book. The source of inspiration for this particular piece is a watercolour made by Sydney Parkinson when he made the 1768-1771 Pacific crossing, accompanying the famous explorer James Cook, and the amateur botanist and collector, Sir Joseph Banks.

By April 1769 the expedition had reached Tahiti where Parkinson painted a garfish. I was amused by the fish's incredible length and thought that it might work well as a mosaic at the same time as cocking a snook at the mackerel shown on p49. The glass fusion used for the eye, right, was chosen to give that particular menace peculiar to garfish.

into their surroundings and often a photograph won't give you all of the information that you need. I find that illustrations are far easier to work from. In fact, it is the job of the natural history illustrator to clarify the very details that a photograph can fall short delivering.

A favourite book of mine is *Voyages of Discovery* by Tony Rice. It shows artworks from three centuries of global voyaging, all of which are taken from the library of the Natural History Museum in London. I would defy anyone not to be impressed by the contents of this book;

many of its drawings and watercolours were made in the most extraordinary circumstances. I heartily recommend it to anyone interested in nature.

Posters, especially those made before the four-colour lithographic printing process came about, are even clearer than colour or black-and-white illustrations. In the old days an illustrator would provide his own overlays, in black and white, for each additional colour. It is very easy to translate these separate overlays into the limited colour palette available to the mosaicist.

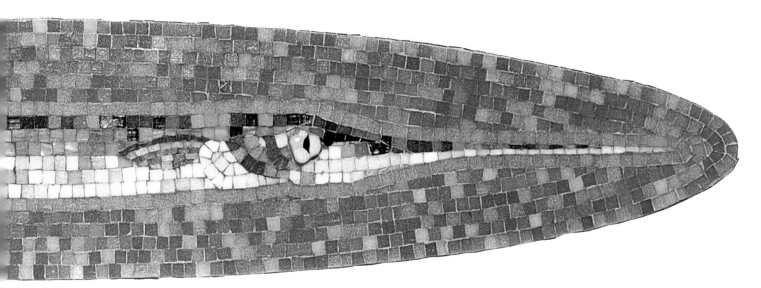

Museums

IN LONDON MY favourite museums are the Victoria & Albert Museum, the British Museum and the Natural History Museum, where I found the pterodactyl, opposite. In America I love the Art Institute of Chicago. Europe has hundreds of wonderful museums and I particularly enjoy the Museé d'Orsay and the Louvre in Paris, the Prado in Madrid, and the Uffizi in Florence.

The first time one visits any museum there is a tendency to run around trying to see everything. Of course, it is important to know the scope and range of the collection, but I find that in trying to see everything one ends up remembering nothing. My method is to take notes on the initial visit and on subsequent visits to concentrate on one subject only.

For example, on my last visit to the Victoria & Albert, I wanted to study their extensive collection of Minton ware. Thanks to this limited personal brief, I didn't feel pressurised into thinking that I was missing any of the other exhibits. I stayed for just over an hour and took in quite a lot, making notes and sketching details as visual reminders where necessary. If I'd stayed six times longer I really believe that I would have probably only have achieved twice as much. I find these short bursts more productive, more enjoyable and more memorable because, 'that was the day that I looked at the Minton.'

Pterodactyl
50cm (19in) diameter, Cinca ceramic, 2000-2001

I love the use of decoration in the architecture of the Natural History Museum in London, which has sadly gone out of fashion. Alfred Waterhouse's design for this magnificent building was made in 1876. It was the first building in England, and possibly in the world, where the main facades were entirely faced with terra-cotta. The facade contains many carved animals, one of which is this striking pterodactyl, and I thought it would be interesting to try and capture it in mosaic.

My personal brief was to 'model' the tones of mosaic so that from a distance the beast looks carved out of stone, like the original on which it is based. This is not as easy as it looks, mainly because when you are working on the mosaic you are sitting over it, only a few inches away, so it looks as though there is plenty of contrast, but when you stand back the mosaic can look very flat.

Consequently, I re-made many of the lines of this piece, which, unlike painting where you simply paint over your mistakes, involves the use of a hammer and chisel to remove the offending tesserae. (Anyone who thinks that the PVA glue, used for sticking the tesserae down when working direct, isn't very strong, soon realizes their error of judgement when they try to remove any pieces.)

I think I got it right in the end – I love the comic menace about him, which reminds me of a Punch and Judy crocodile.

Cathedrals and churches

THESE ARE ALWAYS worth a visit. Irrespective of whether you are religious or not, they still provide a space for quiet reflection. There are many surprises and much inspiration to be found, too, if you take a close look at the floor tiles and brass relief work or at the ceiling bosses, gargoyles and stone carvings. Here are some examples of mosaics worked up from tiles and flooring found on hallowed ground.

All of the mosaics here are inspired by Medieval English tile slabs, often found in churches. This set of slabs all use the same limited palette, which looks like four colours but is actually a few more due to the closeness in shades of the two different makes of ceramic tesserae that I used. The colours match the look of the original old terracotta tiles.

The addition of the gold mirror spots was my idea, meant to add a bit of sparkle and liven up the slabs. These tiles can look a bit flat, so the pieces of mirror, although very few in number, give the slabs depth.

Medieval Knight
49x36cm (19x14in), Cinca ceramic, Astoria ceramic and gold mirror, 2001

This knight was featured on a tile in a medieval pavement that dates from the 13-14th centuries. I liked the way that the shapes had become a bit amorphous (probably from wear over the centuries), so I copied them more or less faithfully when drawing up the design for this mosaic.

Running Rabbit

31x31cm (12x12in), Cinca ceramic, Astoria ceramic and gold mirror, 2001

Like the Hare Table on p106, this rabbit owes a lot to Pisanello's *Vision of St Eustace* in the National Gallery, London. Making the hind leg vertical gives it a more static look, which I thought was more in keeping with the medieval style of this series of mosaics.

Hound

31x31cm (12x12in), Cinca ceramic, Astoria ceramic and gold mirror, 2001

This dog is more stylized than the bloodhound shown below. He's much swifter, more like a greyhound, which is why I've paired him up with the running rabbit, far left.

Hare

31x31cm (12x12in), Cinca ceramic, Astoria ceramic and gold mirror, 2001

This is the companion piece to the hound, far right. They are both from a set of church tiles that depict various hunting scenes.

Sniffing Hound

31x31cm (12x12in), Cinca ceramic, Astoria ceramic and gold mirror, 2001

This looks like the classic stance of the bloodhound about to take the scent of its quarry.

Other artists' work

A PERSONAL STYLE takes time to develop and you can't force it. It will happen gradually or not at all. It has taken me at least twenty years of struggle to get to the point where I feel that what I'm producing is my work and doesn't owe a huge debt to another person's work. Artists are always reluctant to admit that they might owe a debt to another artist.

As a child, I remember that choosing your favourite artist was like choosing your favourite pop star or football team — you were showing your allegiance and championing them all the way. When I was interviewed for art college I was asked the inevitable question, to which my reply was, Ronald Searle. The tutor was so surprised. He told me that the choice was usually a toss up between Salvador Dali and the Pre-Raphaelites! It's easy to see why teenagers might identify with the visual trickery and pyrotechnics of Dali, which on closer inspection is pretty superficial in content, or conversely the dreamy, sugary romanticism of Millais, Holman Hunt and Rossetti. But admiring other artists' work doesn't have to be like being a football fan. Over the years I think that art critics have encouraged a conception of Picasso and Matisse being at the top of Division One, with Léger and Braque following on in Division Two. The truth is it's possible to admire and be in debt to all sorts of artists for all sorts of reasons.

The ceramic work of the Ancient Greek potters looks remarkably modern to me. Every year I run a mosaic and ceramic course on the Candili estate on the island of Evia. A trip to the Archaeological Museum and the Parthenon Museum in Athens is always a highlight. Looking at pots that are three and a half thousand years old is amazing, and these are the ones that just happened to survive. What were the rest of them like?

Cat
30x20cm (12x8in), coloured pencils, 2000, Mollie Cheek

My daughter Mollie was five years old when she drew this cat. I think that it is the so-called 'mistakes' – like the fact that the cat only has three legs and the way that the blue crayon has gone over its chin – that give this drawing such wonderful character and charm. It is indisputably a drawing of a cat; she has really managed to capture something peculiar to that animal. The confidence of her line is incredible, I hope she doesn't lose it and only wish I had it in my work. I had this drawing put onto my mouse mat, which seems appropriate enough.

I love the way that Matisse's work seeks solace from the hubbub of the real world. He must be the only artist to have lived through two world wars and for there to be no sign of that fact whatsoever in his work.

Picasso may be dead, but he won't lie down for many artists. Whenever you try anything new, you realize that he got there first. Pictorially my work has nothing in common with Picasso, but I love the way that he successfully mastered so many mediums.

I admire the work of many bird artists, but Charles Frederick Tunnicliffe (1901-79) and John James Audobon (1785-1851) are streets ahead of most of us: Tunnicliffe for his keen naturalist's observation and Audobon for his wonderful characterisations.

For its exuberance, decadence and for reviving the art of mosaic, I love the Art Nouveau period of 1890-1910. For this short time, everything from the tiniest item of Lalique jewellery to a vast Hector Guimard Parisian metro station entrance had the same stylish design intelligence behind it. Although it didn't and couldn't last for long, Art Nouveau still managed to sweep across the world, only coming to an end with the outbreak of the First World War. Never had the decorative arts been so decorative, nor were they ever likely to be so again.

Contemporary satirical artists such as Ronald Searle and Ralph Steadman and earlier artists such as Otto Dix, George Grosz, Hogarth, Rowlandson and Gilray could all draw brilliantly. Most of us who were academically trained would kill to be able to draw like any of them.

Children's drawings should also be included in this section. I find the freedom of imagination in my own children's drawings amazing. At some point we get told what is right and wrong about our drawings and this is the point at which, it seems to me, we all lose confidence.

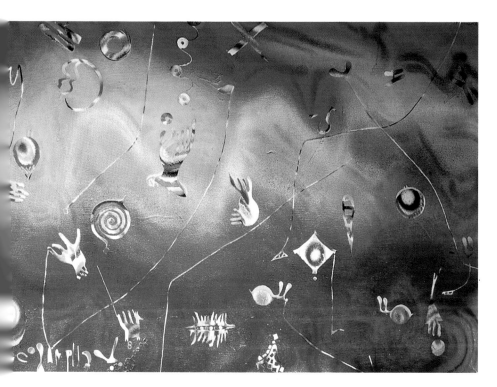

Machynlleth Mela

330×150cm (11×5ft), acrylic paint, 1998, Balraj Khanna
This is the original painting by Balraj Khanna that was specially commissioned by the Museum of Modern Art in Wales with a view to me then making a mosaic of it for the entrance to the museum tabernacle (see p60). Khanna said that he painted this with the medium of mosaic in his mind. It is the same size as the mosaic and I thought that it would be a straightforward job to translate it into mosaic – little did I know!

PART THREE

Mosaics al fresco and indoors

Murals and wall plaques

WALLS DIFFER FROM floors in that with a floor, unless it is for an open courtyard where you can look down upon it from a great height, you are generally going to be looking at it from human head-height. With a wall, the viewer is able to walk back from it and often consider it from a great distance, especially if it is outdoors. The Machynlleth Mela mural for example (see p60) had to make visual sense from across the road at night, lit with spot-lights when the building was closed, as well as at close quarters during the day in natural light. This needs to be borne in mind when you design a wall panel or mural. Where is it going to go? What will be the optimum viewing distance?

I start by making a small scale drawing, say 45x30cm (18x12in) for a 180x120cm (72x48in) mosaic. Once I am happy with this drawing, I photocopy it and draw a grid over it, numbering it across the rows and down the columns: A1, A2, A3, B1, B2, B3, etc. I then copy the grid onto a piece of craft paper the same size I want the finished mosaic to be. I then slavishly copy each square of the small drawing into the corresponding square on the larger sheet. Inevitably there are changes to be made to the larger drawing, dictated by the leap in scale, but at least the proportions are roughly mapped out for you.

A floor needs to be flat in order for people to be able to walk on it, whereas wall panels and murals can be textured and uneven if desired. I love adding pieces of chunky *opus sectile* to my murals, which I feel give it a distinctive style, especially if I have sculpted and raku-fired the elements myself, such as the eye and floral discs on the peacock (see p48).

Cheeky Birds and Cheeky Fish
56cm (22in) diameter, vitreous glass and hand made raku-fired pieces, 2000

See also p50.

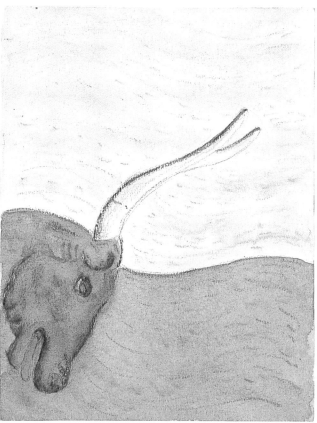

Bull's Head Artwork
30x20cm (12x8in), watercolour and crayon, 2000

This magnificent head is taken from a striking mural at Knossos on the Greek island of Crete. I was impressed by the arch of the back juxtaposed with the angle of the head bearing those wonderful horns. I drew a quick sketch of him on the spot and them worked up this drawing later. I hope that the baking Greek sun is still evident. Crayoning lines over the water-colour once it is dry helps me to imagine what the *opus* of the background will look like when translated into mosaic.

Bull's Head
47x46cm (18½ x18in), Cinca ceramic, 2000

I thought that the rhythm of the background mosaic tesserae when placed *opus musivum* would add something to the quality of this striking image. The choice of Cinca ceramic does make the bull look a bit flat, but I don't mind this as it seems to add to his overall bulkiness. The expression 'taking the bull by the horns' comes from the myth of Theseus, who learned the art of bull leaping from his fellow captives at Knossos.

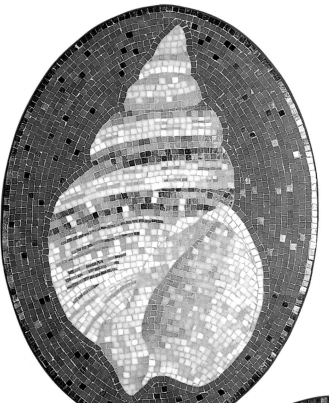

Conch Shell
64x69.5cm (25x27in), vitreous glass and Cinca ceramic, 2000

These shell mosaics work really well from a distance; the brain fuses the various tesserae together to achieve a very realistic effect. I usually try to steer clear of realism, it seems to me to be a never-ending tunnel and once you go down that route, you can go on forever. However, these two shells were so attractive that I thought it would be a challenge, for once, to try and capture them as naturalistically as possible. Also, it's true to say that I'd recently been making lots of mosaics featuring birds and animals and so I fancied a change.

The use of the charcoal matt-black ceramic pushes the background right back to let the shells shine out. I've included a few glass tiles as well, just to add a bit of texture.

'Fox Ear' Conch Shell
64x69.5cm (25x27in), vitreous glass and Cinca ceramic, 2000

It's easy to see why this particular shell is nicknamed the 'fox ear'. The pink inside the actual shell from which this mosaic was taken was the delicious shade of strawberry ice cream.

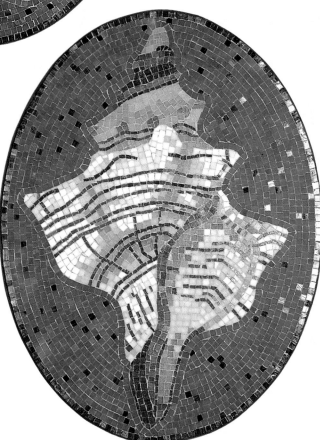

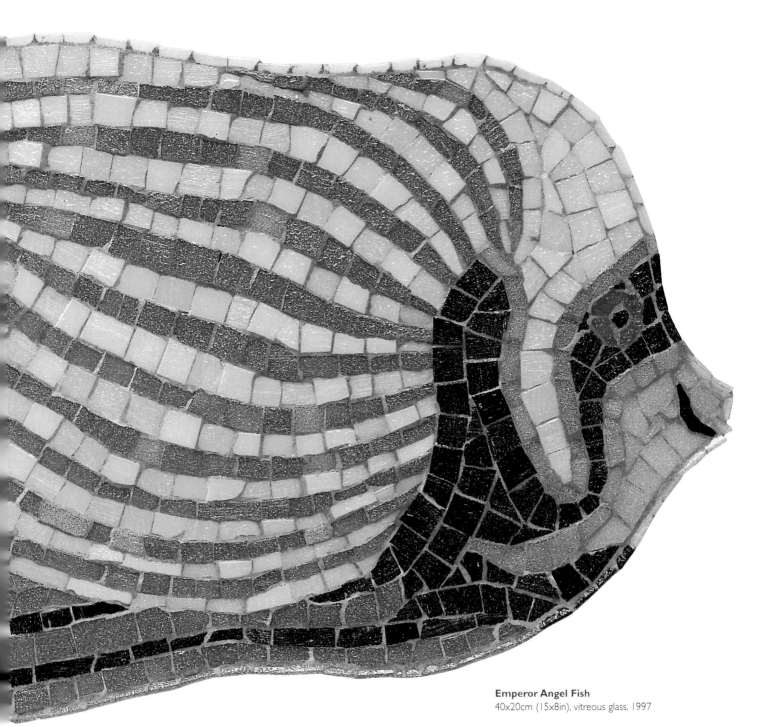

Emperor Angel Fish
40x20cm (15x8in), vitreous glass, 1997

Brightly coloured tropical fish, such as this one, can have amazingly intricate markings. The Emperor's clean blue and yellow stripes have a bold and very graphic feel and are a gift to the mosaic artist. The actual silhouette of fish is equally distinctive, and cutting this simple shape out to make a free-standing plaque has emphasized this.

Peacock
40x86cm (15¾x34in), coloured and gold
leaf smalti and raku-fired pieces, 1998

Smalti is very tricky to work with direct
onto board. I know that this highly prized
glass mosaic was designed to go into wet
plaster, but the plaster gives where board
doesn't. It is a very tedious job to grout a
mosaic made with smalti used direct, as it
requires piece-by-piece attention.
Consequently I try to work extremely
tightly with it, making little or no gaps so
that I can get away without grouting it at
all. However, this in itself is problematic.
So why bother using smalti? Well,
the colour range is not to be
found elsewhere and I do
actually like the texture of the
smalti when used in this way.
The design is inspired by
drawings I made of birds
and a wooden box I
bought in India.

Mackerel
86.5×32.5cm (34×12in), vitreous glass and raku-fired pieces, 1999

I had just finished mosaicing a turbot prior to this piece and the fins had taken me ages to complete. In a fit of what can only be termed sheer laziness, I made a set of fins for this mackerel in raku-fired clay. When I stuck the tiles down on the board they looked most odd, to the extent that I thought that they simply weren't going to work, so I left the mosaic unfinished for many months. Eventually I got sick of seeing it in its unfinished state so I completed it. I was quite surprised to see that when the mosaic completely covered the board it actually worked quite well. Sometimes you just have to trust the process and go along with it.

Greeky Bird
29×32cm (11×12in), vitreous glass, raku-fired pieces and an 'evil eye', 1999

I like my summer course in Greece to somehow reflect the Greek way of life, the Greeks themselves, the climate or natural surroundings. The Greek 'evil eye', intended to ward off evil spirits, was the inspiration for this piece. When I bought it in a nearby village it was meant to be used as a necklace and had a leather strap through it, hence the hole, which conveniently became the bird's ear. With a head like that, the bird had to be a gangly creature, a little like a stork. It also owes a lot to the birds found on ancient Greek pots of the Geometric period, painted 3000 years ago.

Pair of Birds (RIGHT)
32×32cm (12×12in), vitreous glass and raku-fired pieces, 2000

The actual mosaic in this piece is reserved for the background, the subject being made up entirely of ceramic elements used as *opus sectile*. The glaze I used is black when oxidized, but has the sheen of lustreware when reduced (starved of oxygen in the cooling down process).

The inspiration for this work came from an inlaid tile made in the 13-14th centuries. The style is known as the Wessex School and is derived from the tiles in the pavements at Clarendon Palace. Purely by coincidence, I saw a very similar design used as the logo for The Folklore Museum, Naplion, Greece.

Cheeky Bird
31x31cm (12x12in), vitreous glass, 2000

I've used this design a lot, particularly in my ceramic work. Essentially it consists of only three lines, but how those lines are drawn in relationship to each other is vital; the smallest variation can completely change the character of the bird. I like to see how far I can push these basic lines while still getting the characteristics I want.

Cheeky Birds and Cheeky Fish
56cm (22in) diameter, vitreous glass and hand made raku-fired pieces, 2000

I particularly like the pattern formed by the circle of fish. The way that they spiral out gives the mosaic a great sense of movement, like a spinning Catherine Wheel.

Blue Dragon

40.5cm (16in) diameter, vitreous glass, raku-fired pieces, 2000

An example of a mosaic incorporating motifs made and traded on my summer mosaic course. The tear shapes I used to denote the wings and limbs of the dragon were actually made by Wendy, one of the students on the course, who used them as hair in her mosaic of a mermaid. When these hair pieces came out of the raku kiln glowing red and were placed in sawdust to reduce to vivid turquoise, I was

reminded of dragons and so inspired to make this piece.

The square turquoise tesserae used for the body of the dragon were made by rolling out clay, drawing lines on it (rather like a chocolate bar), bisque firing it and then raku-firing the back. The tesserae could then be broken off the sheet in the same way that you break off a piece of chocolate from a bar.

I'm told that if a dragon's tongue is split, then it is Chinese. Certainly, the turquoise colour of the glaze is reminiscent of wonderful Chinese ornaments.

Glass fusions

I MAKE THESE by re-melting bits of smalti. Smalti is very expensive because it is hand made by highly skilled glass-makers, using recipes passed down through generations. At the end of every evening when I was working on the Machynlleth Mela Mural (see p60), I was sweeping up lots of shards of this precious material and throwing it away. I decided to store it and before long I had a row of variously coloured milk bottles lined up on the shelf. When one day my father gave me an old enamelling kiln, last used in the

Fusion Fish
78x40cm (30x15in), vitreous glass, raku-fired ceramic eye and glass fusions, 2000

I made this piece to use up a lot of fusions and thus justify to myself the amount of time that I was spending experimenting with making them. People either love or hate this piece. In retrospect it does look a bit of a hotchpotch; if the fusions had been made out of a limited palette of colours, then they would have given a more harmonious result. That said, it is a good representation of what I was up to at this point in my mosaicing career.

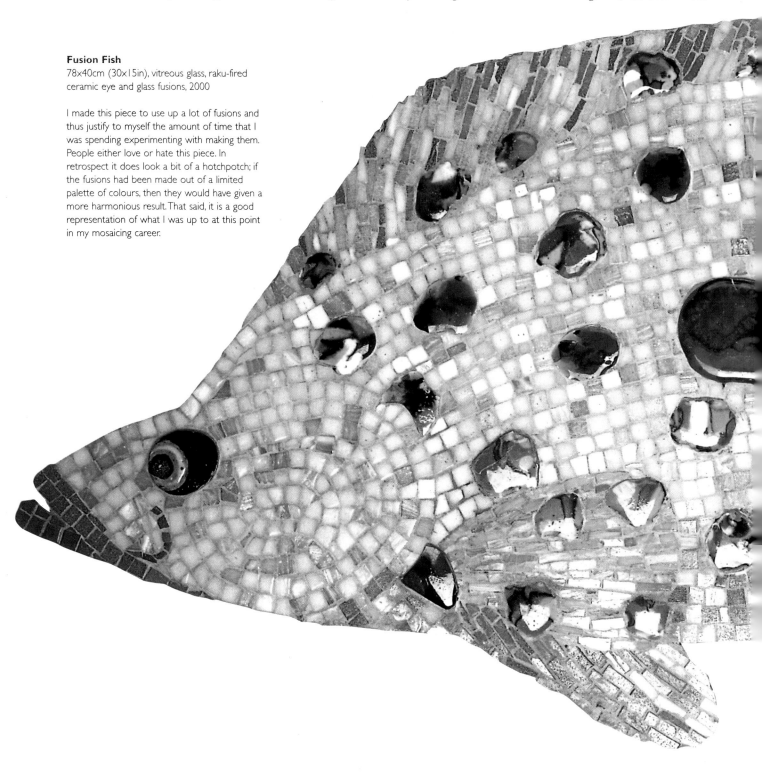

1960s, I thought it would be fun to experiment with the smalti shards. I found that by sprinkling the shards onto bisque-fired ceramic tiles I could re-melt the smalti.

There is very little control over what you get, but I feel that that is all part of the fun. You simply have to make lots more fusions than you need in order to be able to choose the best ones for your mosaics.

Fusion Birds (FOLLOWING PAGES)
Various sizes averaging 22x21cm (8x8in), vitreous glass and glass fusions, 2000

These birds are not 'designed' in any conventional way, but rather created by playing with the fusions until they suggest themselves as a naive bird. I needed a large pool of fusions to choose from and when I thought I'd hit upon an interesting arrangement I drew around the fusions and numbered them so that I could keep moving them around. The amount of mosaic needed to complete each picture varied enormously, as you can see from these examples.

Taliesin Mosaic

Each panel 240x120cm (94½x47in), vitreous glass and natural stone, 1996

This mosaic was the result of a community project with the people of Machynlleth in Wales. The triptych depicts the popular Welsh legend of Taliesin. The action takes place on land, water and air, so the piece was naturally divided up into three panels. I was particularly attracted by the metamorphosis sequence, when the witch, Ceridwen, chases the boy, Gwion. He changes into a hare, so she pursues him in the form of a greyhound; he then transforms himself into a salmon and she into an otter; finally he changes into a bird and she into a bird of prey.

I love trying to put across the individual characters of birds and animals in my mosaic pieces. I found the challenge of trying to capture three completely different animals, each, however, with the same personality, an attractive one.

Land (ABOVE)
The arched shape of each panel was chosen to help the overall flow or *andamento* of the triptych. You can see how the line of action that flows through the hound and hare is emphasized by the curve of the panel itself.

Greyhound (OPPOSITE TOP)
I didn't want the greyhound and the hare to be in the same position in their running cycle. Choosing to have the greyhound with her legs outstretched emphasizes the length and wiriness of the dog and the fact that it runs in long leaps.

Hare (OPPOSITE BOTTOM)
Having the hare with his legs overlapped shows his vulnerability and the way he runs in short gallops. I wanted to show the fear in his eye at the moment at which he looks back to see if he's going to escape.

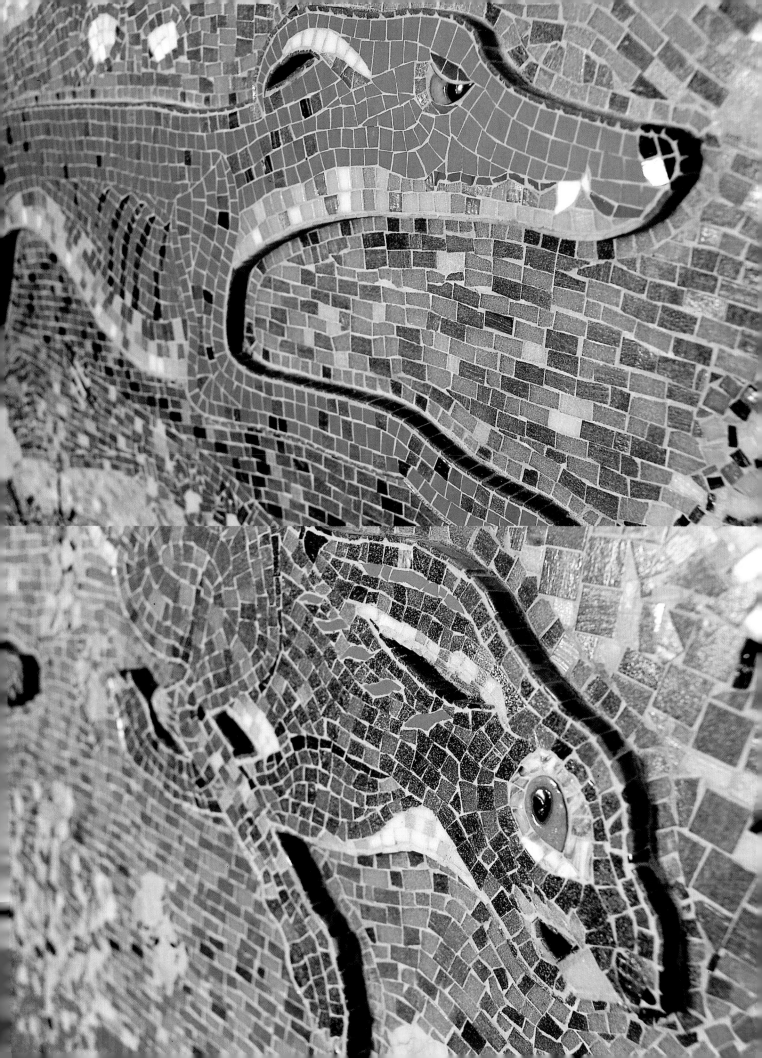

Water
The effect of the water trailing off the salmon and the otter in this middle panel was achieved by combining broken mirror with silver smalti. I used the smalti both ways up, as the reverse is a lovely, vivid blue glass.

Otter
The greyhound, otter and buzzard are all the same character, the witch Ceridwen, in various stages of her metamorphosis. In order to show this I used a palette of browns and ochres for this character throughout the triptych. On this panel the otter's legs are in their back position in her swimming cycle in order to give continuity from the previous piece.

Salmon
Just as the pursuer, Ceridwen, is shown in three guises, so too is the boy, Gwion. I've kept to the same palette of greys and creams for this character. The line of action of the salmon is arched to continue that of the otter; looked at together they form one long arc. This helps the overall *andamento* of the piece, and also explains why this panel is arched in the opposite way to the two adjacent ones.

Air
Susan Goldblatt has a very strong sense of the landscape, which she was able to convey in her design for this background. The sense of flight is emphasized by the view down onto the valley below, as though you, the viewer, are up there with the two protagonists.

Buzzard
The characterisation of this buzzard owes more than a little to a prairie buzzard by one of my favourite wildlife artists, John James Audobon. I suppose if you're going to borrow, you may as well borrow from the best. There are lots of buzzards in Wales, where this legend is set, but I doubt if any of them look like this one.

Swallow
Here I had to break from the palette I had set myself for the boy Gwion. I could have chosen a grey and white bird, such as a rock dove or a pigeon, but I felt that I would have lost some of the drama of the piece. I decided to use a swallow because they are so swift and whereas a pigeon wouldn't stand a chance against a swift raptor, one can be fairly certain that the swallow would be able to dodge its powerful talons.

The Machynlleth Mela Mural

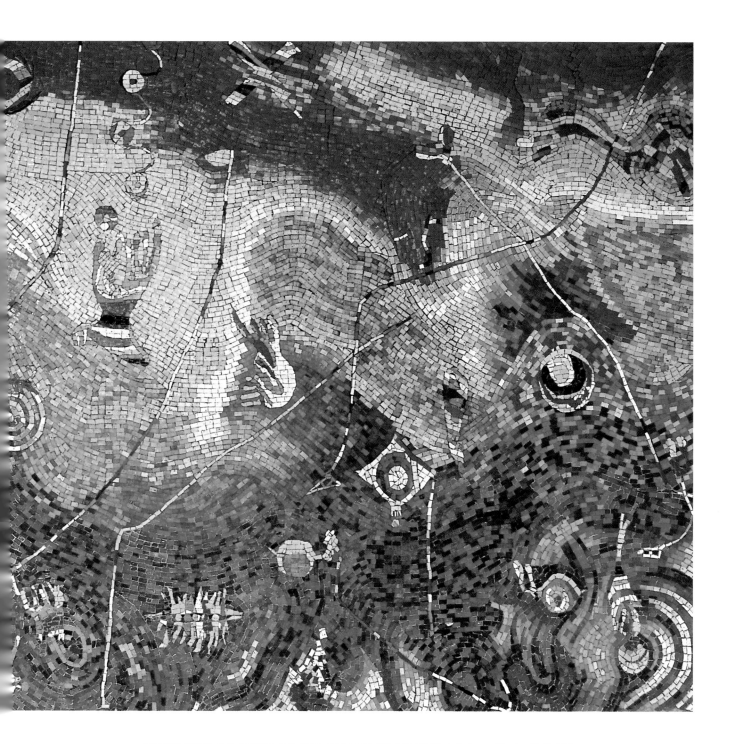

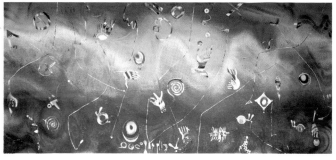

Machynlleth Mela
Mosaic: 330x150cm (132x60in), Venetian smalti, 1998
Painting: 330x150cm (132x60in), acrylic paint, 1998, Balraj Khanna

The large mosaic, above, and the painting which inspired it, left, by Indian artist, Balraj Khanna, were commissioned by the Museum of Modern Art, in Machynlleth. The commission to make a mosaic interpretation of a painting was as unusual as it was demanding.

THIS LARGE PIECE was commissioned by the Museum of Modern Art, in Machynnlleth, the ancient capital of Wales. It now graces the wall of the entrance hall to the auditorium and the aim is to encourage everyone to be in a celebratory mood as they enter.

The Mela is an interpretation of a painting, again specially commissioned by the Museum, by the contemporary Indian artist, Balraj Khanna. His work is known for its calm, meditative qualities and has been likened to the paintings of Joan Miro. The objects in the painting are based on recollections of an exotic childhood in the Punjab. Toys and kites are a crucial part of his subconscious creative thought.

Timeless, joyous, watery images

Abstract painting is always hard to explain, but Khanna's title offers us a clue. A 'mela' is an Indian festival, and the aim of the Machynlleth Mela Mural is to celebrate the performing arts. Some of the objects represent wind chimes and one can imagine the jingle-jangle sounds they would make if they were real. The aim was for the mosaic to capture the timeless, joyous, watery image of Balraj Khanna's original painting. And, of course, the objects can be whatever you interpret them as.

Making the mosaic proved more difficult than I had ever imagined. In the painting, kites, fishing floats, starfish, water creatures, birds, insects, geometrical games and interplanetary vessels spin, rotate, undulate and dart against a soft background. When the painting is viewed from a distance, these brightly coloured objects appear to float in front of the canvas; they hover like fish in an aquarium, or fluttering birds in an aviary. How could one create that effect with pieces of coloured glass?

Normally, I mosaic a line of background colour around each object: this is the Roman technique known as *opus vermiculatum*. When I tried it here, however, it spoilt the overall *andamento* of the piece. Clearly, the background had to 'crash' through the objects. I soon learned that we had to treat the ribbons as kite strings – in other words, they should not disturb the background. Changing the flow on either side of a ribbon made it look like a boat's wake through water. We wanted the same effect as that of a kite string on the air – none! Placing exactly the same colour on either side of the ribbons helped to achieve this.

In terms of tone

We had constantly to think in terms of tone. It was possible to use many colours on the same flow line as long as they were tonally the same. To establish the tone, we had to ask ourselves whether, if we took a black-and-white photocopy, the colours would be the same shade of grey. Adding colours of vastly different tone made the lighter ones sing out and ideally, the viewer should not be aware of the background at all. If you compare it to the stars in

(LEFT AND OPPOSITE) Details taken from different areas of this large piece. Choice of colours is one of the most important aspects about any mosaic – notice how by adding colours of vastly different tone, the lighter ones sing out.

the sky, the background is the sky. It was important to consider the 'weight' of the area one was working on. Darker colours are heavier and all the weight is at the bottom of the picture. If we had used colours that were too light at the bottom, then we wouldn't have had anything left to say in the middle.

Beloved smalti

Once we were happy with the interpretation of the painting, the first thing I had to do was to try and calculate how much material I would require. It was agreed that I should use smalti, the handmade Venetian glass beloved by the Byzantines and every other mosaic artist since. Smalti bought in this country has a range of 87 different colours and is very expensive. However, it is about half the price if bought directly from the factory, which made me realize that it would be worth going to Venice and choosing the smalti myself.

In Venice they can offer about 5,000 colours and they will make up any other colours required. This was good

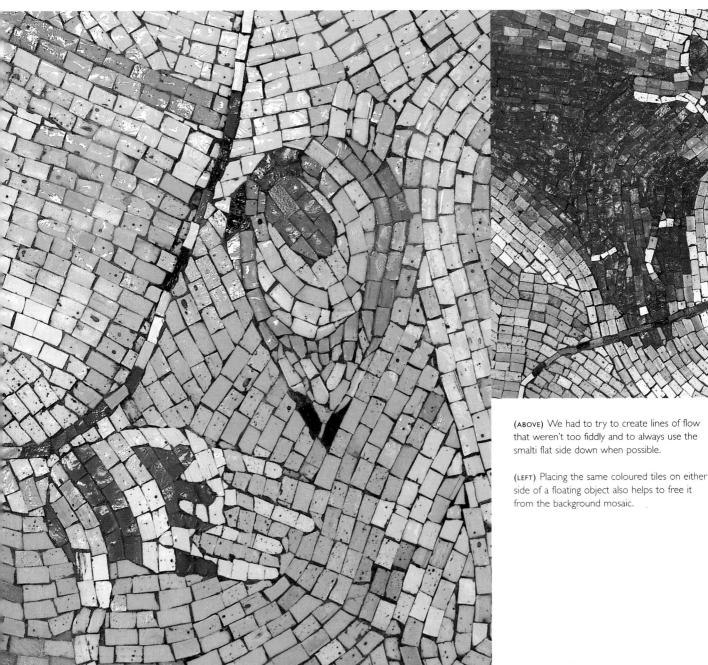

(ABOVE) We had to try to create lines of flow that weren't too fiddly and to always use the smalti flat side down when possible.

(LEFT) Placing the same coloured tiles on either side of a floating object also helps to free it from the background mosaic.

news, because although 87 colours sounds a lot, there are not many bright primaries, and the rich reds, yellows and blues in Khanna's painting are what gives it such superb resonance. In order to make the selection, I photographed the painting in great detail, making up a photo montage to take with me to Venice.

The mosaic was worked indirect onto brown craft paper using water-soluble wallpaper paste. This mosaic was to be divided up into between 50 and 60 sheets, each one approximately 30cm (1ft) square. This took us six months to complete. The mosaic was then installed on site by 'buttering' each piece and applying it to the rendered wall following registration lines and numbers on the back of the sheets. Not being a fixer myself, we called on the help of the architect's builder to render the wall and 'butter' the segments. It took two days to carry out the enormous task of grouting and cleaning the 5 square metres (55 square feet) of finished mosaic. The entire project was finished and installed in time for the 1998 Machynlleth festival.

(LEFT) By crashing the background through the ribbons they appear to float in space without disturbing the mosaic around them.

(BELOW) It was the tonal values rather than the colours themselves that were important in the background. The variety of hues didn't matter as long as they were of the same tone.

(BELOW) Where colour did come into more consideration was with its 'weight'. Darker colours are heavier looking and so had to be used at the bottom of the picture, with light colours at the top.

Floors and floor slabs

THE MOST IMPORTANT thing to say about floors is that they need to be durable and they need to be flat. For this reason I always work indirect when making a floor mosaic. Vitreous glass isn't really an option, as anyone walking on it with high heels could crack it. Cinca ceramic is ideally suited for floors and is used extensively in Spain and Portugal. It is suitable for indoors and outdoors, but make sure that you use an exterior adhesive for outdoors.

If you intend the mosaic to go outdoors, consider how far away the viewer will be. A large space can play strange tricks with the size of your mosaic and it may be worth scaling up your design to suit the space. The tits in the Wildlife Courtyard mosaic (see p74) averaged 21x16cm (8x6in) in size, but when viewed from a distance, appeared to be about the actual size of the real birds.

Similarly, if the mosaic is intended for a small, enclosed indoor area, remember that the viewer will be standing over it and looking down on it from head height. Test out your design by placing it on the floor and walking round it.

It is also worth remembering that the mosaic will simply form a skin on the existing floor, it won't make it flat; the floor surface must be perfectly flat before you start. Remember also that mosaic has no structural strength, in fact, quite the opposite – it is made up of a lot of small pieces, so mosaicing a weak floor won't strengthen it. If in doubt it is worth asking a builder to check the foundations of the floor and confirm that it is strong enough to take a mosaic.

The idea of mosaicing an entire terrace may seem daunting, but you don't have to mosaic the whole area. Even if you only manage a simple border or a centrepiece and fill in the rest with sheets of uncut tiles, it will still make the space special. Many Roman mosaics have *emblemata*, a central panel that is often the most highly worked part. These are usually pictorial and offer a contrast to the surrounding geometric or abstract patterns and borders.

**Leisure Centre
Directional Slabs**
61x61cm (24x24in),
Cinca ceramic, 2000

See also p86.

Eagle Floor

This multiple design with eagles shows the arms of Richard of Cornwall, the founder of the Cistercian Abbey of Hailes. The original floor of inlaid tiles is from Hailes Abbey in Gloucestershire and was made for Anthony Melton who was the Abbot from 1509-1527. I made the floor as a series of slabs because I wanted to keep the look of the original tiles. The tiles didn't match perfectly, which I really liked and I wanted to try and keep that quirky quality in these mosaics.

Eagle Floor Artwork
Watercolour, 2001

Before embarking on the Eagle Floor, I thought that I'd better draw it up to make sure that it worked. I actually preferred this watercolour when it was half finished, as a work in progress.

Tile 1
This tile sits in the corners of the floor.

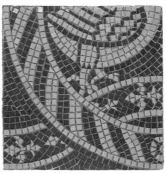

Tile 2
One of the two tiles depicting the eagles' talons.

Tile 3
The difference between this tile and tile two is subtle, but vital to the composition.

Tile 4
This tile makes up the centre section of the floor.

Eagle Floor

124x124cm (51x51in), Cinca ceramic and
Astoria ceramic, 2001

Though the completed floor looks complicated,
it is, in fact, made up from only four tiles, each of
which is used four times.

Look at the diagram, right, and you will see
exactly how the single tiles, opposite, fit together
to form the whole design.

1	3	2	1
2	4	4	3
3	4	4	2
1	2	3	1

Old English Tile Floor
62x62cm (25x25in), Cinca ceramic and Astoria ceramic, 2001

This is simply another version of the Eagle Floor (see p68), using only the corner slab repeated four times to make a circle. I can imagine this in the middle of a large floor or courtyard. It just goes to show that even if you only have the time or money for a small mosaic, it can still make a big difference if it is placed as a centrepiece in a room.

Naquada Ram

IN UPPER EGYPT a new culture emerged shortly after
4000BC, known as the Naquada culture. Most influential of
all the pre-dynastic cultures, it produced in its final stages
the kings who were to unify the disparate peoples of Upper
and Lower Egypt.

This mosaic is inspired by one of the cosmetic palettes
in the form of animals, which were commonly made by the
Naquada people around 4000-3600BC. I found this one in
the British Museum, but I've seen wonderful examples
elsewhere, notably at the Ashmolean Museum in Oxford.
They are made of basalt, a hard stone that could be
worked and polished into primitive animal shapes.

Naquada Ram
41x38cm (16x15in), sand and
cement slab, marble, flint eye,
2001

I wanted this mosaic to reflect
the ancient inspiration, so
marble seemed the obvious
choice. I love the subtle
variation in the marble, which
when cut up into tesserae and
reassembled, gives the mosaic
its soft quality. I collect flint
from the beach, and used a
particularly 'beady' piece for
the eye.

I didn't want to mosaic a
background, preferring to keep
it as simple as possible. I just
made a wooden mould
around it and poured sand and
cement on it. I coloured the
cement with a red cement
dye, available from builders'
merchants, in order to make it
look more Egyptian. For once I
was really pleased with the
result. It's funny how I'm often
dissatisfied with a complicated,
ambitious mosaic, which never
quite seems to live up to my
expectations, while a naive
simple piece like this seems
to succeed.

Wildlife Courtyard

WE DIDN'T WANT to cover the entire courtyard in mosaiced animals because it would have been overwhelming. Instead I provided a 'shopping list' of flora and fauna with their respective sizes and price. From this list my client was able to tick off the ones she wanted and easily stick to her budget.

Each item was treated as a sort of sticker; I would mosaic it and the row of background tiles delineating it – the *opus vermiculatum*. Complete sheets of plain tiles were then used to fill in most of the background and finally tiles were cut to fit around each 'sticker', so it looked as though the subject had been dropped into the plain tiles. The mosaics were made indirect and the entire job was delivered on craft paper stretched over boards, ready to be placed around the courtyard and laid along with the sheets of plain tiles.

My client's bedroom window overlooked this courtyard. When it was finished she told me that she took great pleasure in looking out of a morning and seeing the real birds flying down to intermingle with the mosaic ones around the central bird bath.

Pair of Hares
Jack (RIGHT), 50x99cm (19x39in); Jill (BELOW),
54x80cm (21x31n); Cinca ceramic, 2000

These hares are not two males fighting, but
rather a Jill rejecting a Jack because she hasn't
come into season yet. I wanted to emphasize
their length, which is much greater than that of
a rabbit. I was particularly pleased with the line
of action in the Jack, which runs down his left
ear, along his nose, through his right arm and
into his left leg. The three colours of white,
cream and buff on his tummy are meant to
suggest the light of a strong summer's day.

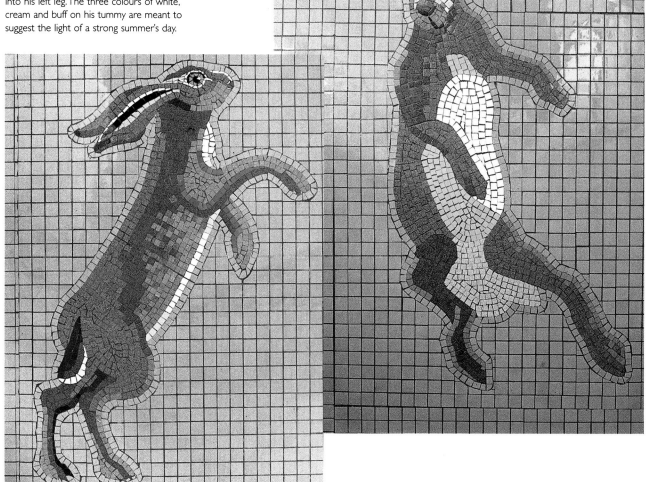

Grass Snake
46x68cm (18x26in), Cinca ceramic, 2000

Placing this snake so that he is hiding under a
lavender bush was inspired. He really looks as
though he belongs there, basking in the sun. The
colours used on the body are fairly neutral,
allowing the beady eye and yellow neck stripe
to sing out.

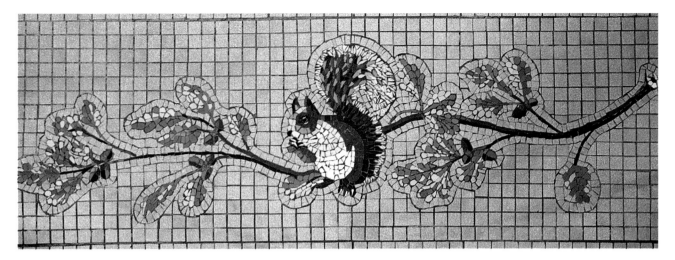

Squirrel and Oak Branch
123x34cm, (48x13in), Cinca ceramic, 2000

Although considered a pest in commercial woodlands, as they do so much damage to valuable trees, squirrels are much loved elsewhere because their behaviour is so attractive and endearing. Personally I blame Beatrix Potter for creating the adorable Squirrel Nutkin. I used the same design for this squirrel as for the Wildlife Table (see p90). Lazy of me I know, but then again, if something works, don't change it. I thought that the grey shards making up the silvery, bushy tail were particularly successful. The oak leaves work well, especially considering that they are entirely made up of only two shades of green.

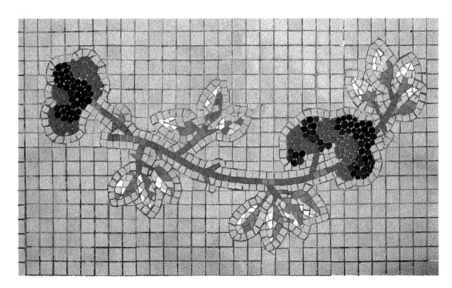

Blackberries
101x22cm (39x8in), Cinca ceramic, 2000

The blackberry or bramble must be one of the most familiar free foods in British hedgerows. Two thousand species have been recorded and brambles in one area can look totally different from those in another. Legend has it that blackberries should not be eaten after Michaelmas (September 29) because the Devil then spits on them. This is actually good advice – the fruit becomes mushy and insipid at about that time of year.

Cutting a circle in mosaic is tricky at the best of times, but nibbling all of those tiny circles as small as possible to make the berries convincing took an enormous amount of time and patience, as you can probably imagine.

Elderberries
82x32cm (32x12in), Cinca ceramic, 2000

Man has cultivated the elder for centuries. The fruit and flowers make excellent wines and jams, rich in Vitamin C. More relevant to me, however, was the way I was able to capture this branch in mosaic by cutting out each one of the clusters of tiny round berries.

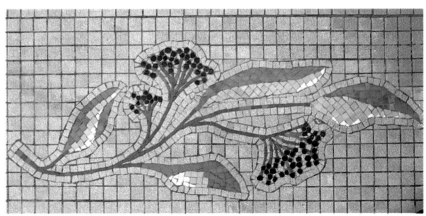

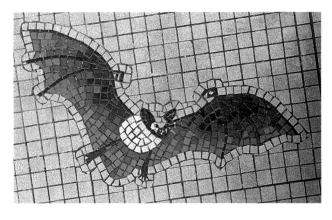

Three Bats
Average 46x30cm (18x11in), Cinca ceramic, 2000

There are nineteen families of bats throughout the world but only two, horseshoe bats and ordinary bats, are found in Britain. Most people dislike bats – probably because of their long association with Count Dracula – but in fact they are harmless and very interesting creatures. When staying on the Candili estate in Greece, I love to swim in the pool at night. The bats are there, too, and to witness them swooping and narrowly avoiding obstacles thanks to their echo-location systems is a spectacular sight.

It was quite difficult to try to suggest the thin membrane of the wings compared to the soft furry tummies. We managed to capture that look of menace on their faces, though.

Spider
42x39cm (16x15in), Cinca ceramic, 2000

I had to enlarge this spider to many times its real size in order to try to capture the delicacy of the legs: the tesserae used for them were about 3mm (⅛in) wide. Changing the colour of these tesserae suggests variation in the thickness as the visual 'weight' of the darker colours makes them look heavier than the lighter ones. The *opus vermiculatum* is absolutely essential in this case; if the background tiles had simply crashed straight into the legs, the whole mosaic would have looked a total mess.

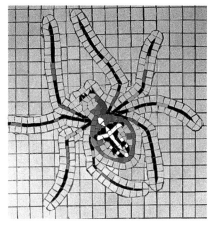

Mother and Baby Hedgehog (OPPOSITE)
41x33cm (16x13in), Cinca ceramic, 2000

The hedgehog is Britain's only spiny mammal. An adult hedgehog has some 50,000 spines on its back, so it required lots of spiky tesserae to represent their prickly coats. These were layered in circular rows, starting from the neck and spanning outwards along their backs. Their facial expressions do seem to capture the hedgehog's mischievous quality.

Pheasant
88x52cm (34x20in), Cinca ceramic, 2000

The pheasant is Britain's most widespread game bird. Although they can't fly very far, pheasants can rise steeply and very quickly when danger threatens, and it always takes me by surprise to see one shoot out of the undergrowth when I'm driving through the English countryside. The pheasant's natural home, however, is Asia, and those with a white neck-ring, like the one shown here, were brought to England from China in the 17th century. I used the same drawing that I had used previously for the Wildlife Table (see p90), but you can see what a difference the change of medium – from vitreous glass to Cinca ceramic – has made. This one looks far more naturalistic, but I think I prefer the gaiety of the brightly coloured, shiny glass bird.

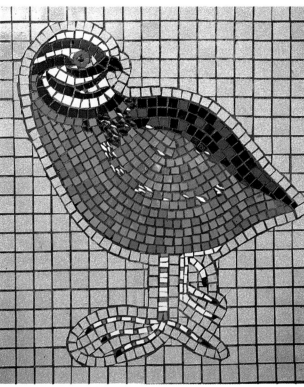

Quail
40x46cm (15x18in), Cinca ceramic, 2000

I make lots of ceramic quails because I love their plump form. They are reluctant to fly and are only usually seen when flushed from the meadows. The mottled neck and the streaked back translated well into this mosaic. I was able to capture the detail because I enlarged him to about three times his actual size.

Nuthatch
44x29cm (17x11in), Cinca ceramic, 2000

The nuthatch is the only bird that can hop down tree trunks as easily as it hops up. The name is derived from his original name, the 'nut-hack', because of this bird's trick of fixing nuts into a crevice in tree bark and hacking them open with its bill. I wanted to emphasize its dagger-like bill, which is why I swept the line of action straight down the bird's back, along the black eye-stripe and into the bill. I have exaggerated the blue on his back, which should be a blue-grey, but I wanted to brighten up the courtyard.

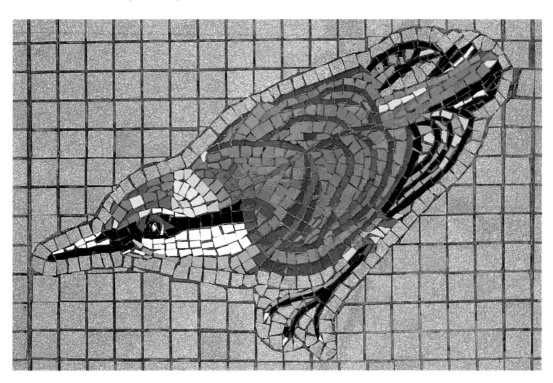

Blackbird
34x50cm, (13x19in),
Cinca ceramic, 2000

A watercolour by Charles Frederick Tunnicliffe inspired this mosaic. I know that the blackbird should really be all black and that this one has a lot of blue on his tail and wing, but how else was it possible to describe his form?

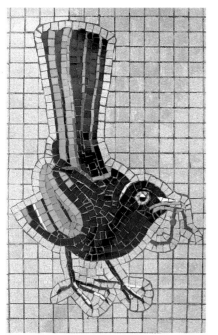

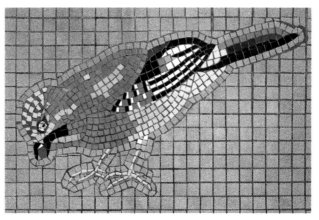

Jay
55x33cm (21x13in), Cinca ceramic, 2000

The jay is in fact a member of the crow family, although you wouldn't guess this. It is a wary bird and is more often heard than seen. They are fond of acorns, so I decided to show this one collecting one to bury later among fallen leaves and twigs. The crest was hard to depict and the result looks more chequered than streaked.

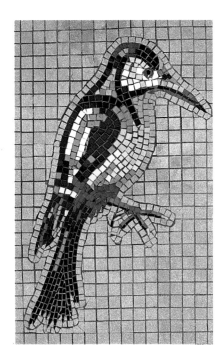

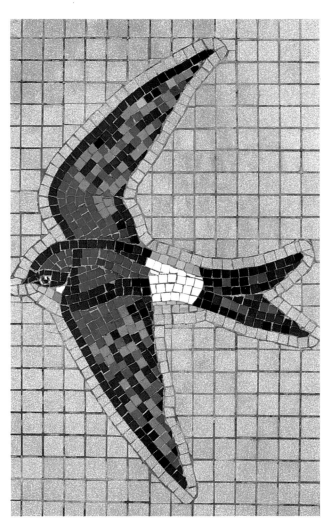

Great Spotted Woodpecker
39x59cm (15x23in), Cinca ceramic, 2000

It's usually the characteristic drumming that gives
away the presence of this bird, as he makes a
series of rapid blows to a dead bough or
telegraph pole with his strong, sharp bill.

House Martin
39x56cm (15x22in),
Cinca ceramic, 2000

The adult house
martin has pure
white underpants
and the upper parts
are mainly blue-black.
I wanted to show
him from above,
soaring through the
air. I played down the
black because I didn't
want my martin to
be too heavy. I
substituted two
tones of grey, which I
think works, so long
as you concede that
you are looking at
him in strong light.

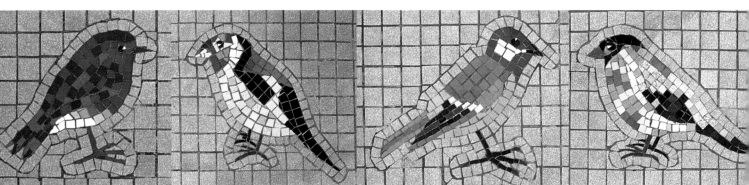

(FROM LEFT)

Robin
18x17cm (7x6in), Cinca ceramic, 2000

The robin is Britain's best-loved bird, noted for
its tameness in town and city gardens. It will
often search for food around the feet of
gardeners who are turning over the soil. My
mosaic robin is plumper than a real one, but I
wanted to emphasize his pugnacious cuteness.
Unlike tits, robins seem to prefer breadcrumbs.

Goldfinch
24x23cm (9x9in), Cinca ceramic, 2000

A flock of goldfinches is called a 'charm' and
there is no better way of describing these birds.

Great Tit
25x22cm (9x8in), Cinca ceramic, 2000

In old Icelandic, the word *tittr* meant a small bird
or anything small, so our corruption of it
provided a fitting name for members of the tit

family. The great tit is the largest of these and
also the most acrobatic.

Bullfinch
25x19cm (9x7in), Cinca ceramic, 2000

The bullfinch is unmistakable with his red
underpants, black cap, grey upper parts and
startling white rump.

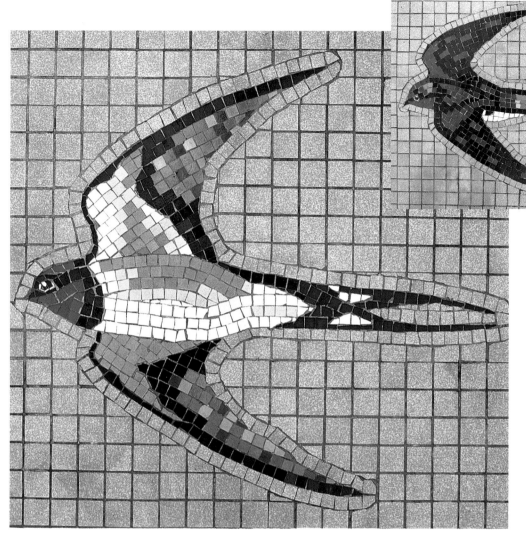

Two Swallows

Average 48x42cm (18x16in),
Cinca ceramic, 2000

I find it impossible to look at a swallow without being reminded of Oscar Wilde's fairy story, *The Little Prince*. The swallow has a longer tail than the house martin and I wanted to emphasize this in these two mosaics. When in flight swallows change directions constantly, darting back and forth. Last year I witnessed one coming straight at me as I stood in an outdoor swimming pool; it was swooping for a drink before soaring back heavenwards. It was this dynamism that I was trying to capture here.

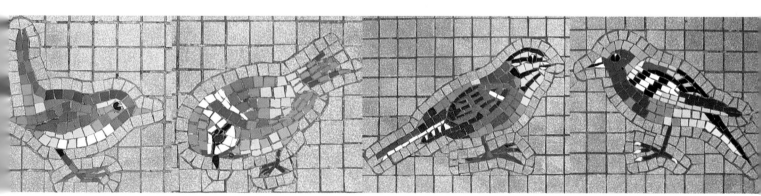

Wren

18x19cm (7x7in), Cinca ceramic, 2000

The tiny wren with his cocked tail should have been the most difficult to handle in mosaic, but I think that this study is the most successful of all of the ones of the small birds shown here. Notice how only five white tesserae are used to highlight his breast.

Blue Tit

21x16cm (8x6in), Cinca ceramic, 2000

The blue tit can be identified by its bluish upper parts and yellow underpants. The white face with its bright blue crown is very distinctive. As we all know, they like coconuts.

Yellowhammer

28x18cm (11x7in), Cinca ceramic, 2000

This is the bird that supposedly sings 'a-little-bit-of-bread-and-no-cheese.' The eggs are white or purplish white with bold scribblings, thus the yellowhammer has the alternative name of 'scribble lark'.

Chaffinch

25x19cm (9x7in), Cinca ceramic, 2000

The chaffinch has a beautiful slate-blue crown and neck, which along with its chestnut back, pinkish underpants and greenish rump, make it easy to identify.

Underwater Panel

This mosaic was commissioned under the 'percentage for art' scheme, whereby a local council encourages part of the money given for a redevelopment project to be spent on an accompanying work of art.

The brief was to design a work that would be harmonious with its surroundings (in this case, a shopping mall) and not so loud as to distract from the building's river setting. Andrew Higgins and I both put in different designs, in our own styles, and Andrew's was the one chosen, with a few minor changes.

The design I put forward was one that I eventually made as the Cheeky Birds and Cheeky Fish panel (see p50). Obviously, if it had been chosen it would have had to be made as a flat mosaic, without any of the *opus sectile* pieces that I used in the panel.

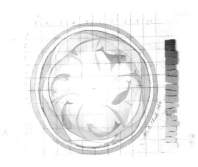

Underwater Panel Artwork
28cm (11in) diameter, watercolour and pencil on watercolour paper, 2000, Andrew Higgins

My friend Andrew Higgins and I both submitted designs for this commission. This is the one that was chosen. Being beaten by my former student was a painful blow to my fragile ego, but Andrew has done this so many times that I have had to get used to it! There is a delicacy in Andrew's watercolours that is hard to recreate in ceramic tesserae, but we did our best.

Drawing a grid over the artwork and scaling it up to actual size has become standard practice for me. Having plotted out the design, it is still usually necessary to make a few adjustments to allow for the change in scale.

Sticking down a 'palette' of tiles alongside the artwork is a good idea as you can see at a glance the colours you need.

Underwater Panel
200cm (78in) diameter, Cinca ceramic, 2000

The effect that we were trying to achieve here is of being under the water and looking up at the sun shining on the surface above you. The concentric circles greatly help by drawing your eye to the centre. The way that these were kept in line was by using a strip of wood pivoting from the centre of the circle. The beginning of each row could then be marked off as we worked inwards.

I decided that an *opus vermiculatum* round the reeds and the fish would interfere with the regularity of the background so instead we simply 'crashed' the background tiles into them. The use of whole, uncut tiles for the background was chosen to give a contrast in size and to create a regularity in the background. By the time we got to the white middle section, the tiles had to be slightly tapered into wedges, so as not to leave any triangular gaps in between them.

Leisure Centre Mosaics

This was quite a tricky commission to design, given that it had to include all the activities that the centre had to offer: badminton, tennis, table tennis, football, basketball and netball, as well as a sauna, gym and massage facilities. With all of that going on, it would have been too easy to have a cluttered and messy result. Together Andrew Higgins and I pared it down to show the racket sports by simply having a hand holding a racket, and the rest followed suit.

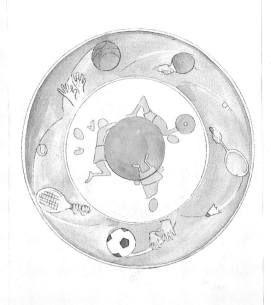

Leisure Centre Activities Artwork
28cm (11in) diameter, pencil and watercolour, 2000

If you look at the initial design you will see that we changed the colour of the table tennis bat from red to green in order to evenly distribute these two colours. The clean blue used for the outer circle allows the objects to stand out. It was important that the two shades of darker blue, used to 'pepper' the background and add texture, did not touch the objects.

Leisure Centre Directional Slabs
61x61cm (24x24in), Cinca ceramic, 2000

The intended car park for the leisure centre is a short walk away along a pathway made of herringboned bricks. It was feared that some people might not be able to find their way to the centre, so I had the idea of laying these directional slabs in the existing herringbone pattern. Each slab covers the area of nine bricks, so fixing the slabs was simply a matter of removing the existing bricks and replacing them with a single slab.

The 'whiz' lines are very much in the graphic tradition of comic books. I drew them very quickly, pivoting the arc from the elbow, as opposed to the wrist, and wanted to make sure that the mosaics kept that look of spontaneity. In this case I did feel that an *opus vermiculatum* would help to delineate the white flash lines from the buff background.

Leisure Centre Activities Mosaic
200cm (78in) diameter, Cinca ceramic, 2000

A circle was an obvious choice for the overall shape, as it works from all angles and directions. The figures in the middle are semi-abstract – they are not meant to be too specific, or even anatomically correct. I didn't want to get into

any debate about the sizes and shapes of people's bodies and neither did I want to show any preference for race, hence the neutral yellow-ochre colours of the figures.

The middle band of white breaks the concentric pattern of the rest of the background. The swirling was supposed to represent steam (or sweat) and while this doesn't

necessarily read as such, I still think that it was important to break the regularity of the background in this area.

Tables

AN OBVIOUS BUT important question to ask yourself when designing a table is, 'What will it be used for?'. If it is a large, outdoor table to be used on special occasions by a dozen or so people, such as the Wildlife Table (see p90), then it needs to look good with nothing on it. However when the time comes and cutlery and glasses are laid on it, along with all the bowls and dishes of food, then special considerations are needed in order for the table not to look too cluttered, or at worst, a complete mess.

If the table is going to be used as a kitchen table, with everyday clutter on it most of the time, then a cleaner, less fussy approach would be more suitable. A simple geometric border with a plain design in the middle can look fantastic.

Is the table going to be used as a practical table or purely as a decorative piece? The chances are that it's the former, in which case it will need to be flat. When mosaicing a table I always work indirect onto paper to ensure that the finished mosaic will have a flat surface.

Ready-made tables are an ideal choice to mosaic. Mosaicing over a rusty metal table top is a good way of salvaging it. Even the tattiest second-hand pine table can be stripped down, painted and its top brought to life with a lovely bright mosaic.

Nautilus Shell tabletop
129x129cm (51x51in),
Cinca ceramic, 2000

See also p102.

Wildlife Table

335½×152cm (132×60in), vitreous glass, 1998

THE BRIEF WAS to make an outdoor dining table that a dozen people could comfortably sit around. The problem with a large circular table is that no one can reach the middle; mosaics are easy enough to clean but you have to be able to get to them. Besides which, I didn't think that a huge circular table would look as impressive as an elliptical one. A normal person can reach just over 70cm (27in) to 'pass the salt', so that length doubled determined the width of the table.

The inspiration for this work was the local flora and fauna of Berkshire. The client was familiar with my work and simply said, 'Surprise me!' I was given a completely free hand to carry out the work as I saw fit. It is very unusual to have such freedom and demands a lot of trust from the client, so it was a joy to be commissioned by someone who really understood and appreciated my work. I work a lot these days in conjunction with a blacksmith, Julian Coode of Nailbourne Forge in Canterbury; he designed the metalwork and I designed the mosaic.

It was also an important consideration to balance the colour throughout the piece. In other words, not having all the bright colours together but distributing them evenly around the table. I find that it helps to think of colour in terms of its 'weight' – dark, bright colours being 'heavier' than soft, pale ones. When thought of in this sense, the use of the word 'balance' makes perfect sense.

My client and I both wanted the mosaic to be bright, colourful and to shine in the summer sunlight. Thus vitreous glass was the obvious choice in this case, but if you turn to p74, you will see similar designs rendered in ceramic. These mosaics were for a courtyard floor and were meant to complement the natural colours of the flowers and shrubs in the garden; so in that instance ceramic was the better option.

Squirrel and Oak Branch
I used grey veined tiles to try to emulate the squirrel's bushy tail.

Hare
This pose seems to show the alertness of the brown hare, their heads are never down for long even when feeding. I wanted to emphasize its length, which is surprisingly long at 56cm (22in) with its spindly, yet powerful legs. Its triangular shape is meant to reflect that of the fox at the opposite end of the table.

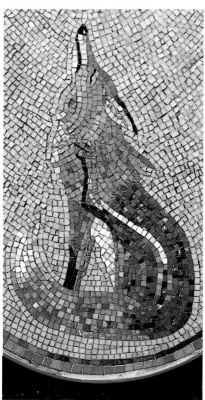

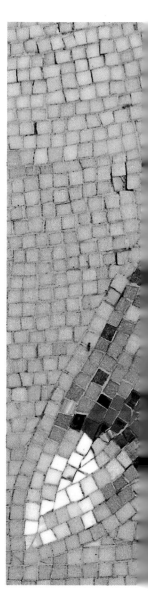

Fox
The fox, stretching upwards and scratching his chin, makes a strong vertical line. The overall shape is a cone that reaches up and points along the major axis to the hare at the opposite end of the table.

Designing the birds and animals

An overall design consideration for this table was to make sure that such a large area didn't become fragmented by all of the separate elements on it; clearly they need to visually link up. To achieve this, I not only designed the animals as individual mosaics, but also as complementary elements within the ellipse. It helps a lot if you visualize the major and minor axis running through the ellipse (see diagram on p98). The fox, kestrel, barn owl and hare all link up visually along the major axis. If you don't believe me, cover any one of them with your hand and see what happens.

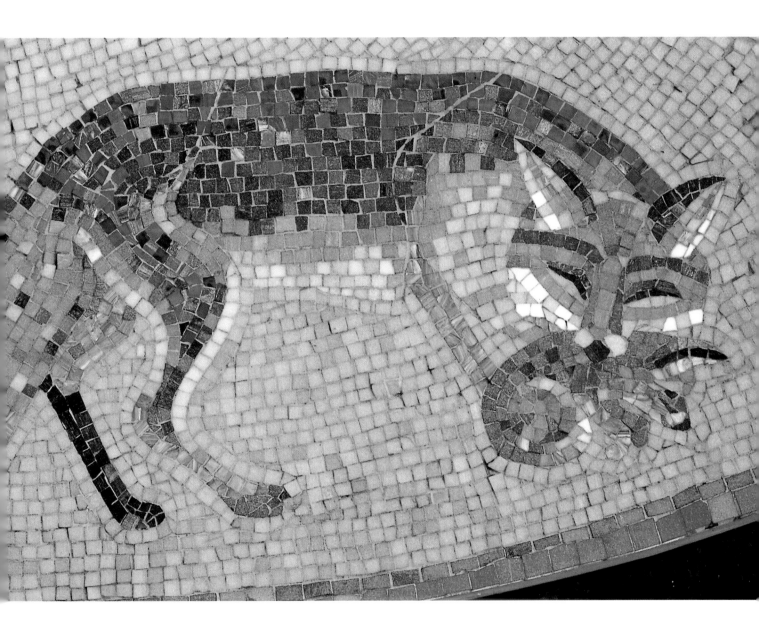

Vixen Carrying Her Cub
There are only three bright orange tesserae on the vixen's back, yet they really stand out. Three out of thirty-five thousand might not sound many, but they are necessary in order to tie in with the bright colours on the pheasant. It was quite difficult trying to define the face of the cub in such a small area, and simplify it enough so that it was distinct from its mother.

Badgers

I was particularly pleased with this group. Making each badger distinct from the other was a challenge given the limited palette – the addition of dark purple helped to achieve this.

There are three different whites available, all of which can be distinctly seen here. The greyish one only obtains its grey tone after grouting, this is because it is translucent and the grey grout gives it colour.

You can see that only three legs are visible. Any more legs and the composition would be cluttered – while fewer would be impertinence.

Barn Owl

I extended the wings beyond their natural length in order to reach along the table and make a visual line from the hare through the owl, via the kestrel, to the fox. The way the face is modelled in two halves is quite successful. If you look at the skull of a barn owl it's surprising to see that most of that head is made up of soft downy feathers.

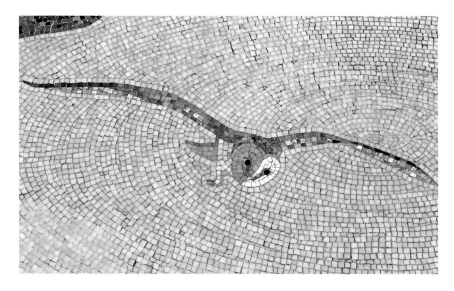

Kestrel

This hovering kestrel, though small, plays a vital part in visually linking the owl to the fox. I didn't want to have two birds of a similar size with their wings outstretched, so making this one smaller seemed to be the best solution.

Pheasant

Mosaic is an ideal medium to show off the chequered markings of this beautiful bird. When you spot a pheasant in the wild it seems huge and very, very long. I can never quite equate this majestic bird with the chubby fowl that is to be found on the supermarket shelf.

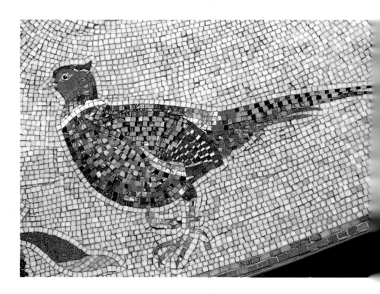

Background

Throughout the mosaic it was very important that the background colour should be soft and not clash or interfere with the strong palette of the animals. The pale green, which gradually filters into a blue is, of course, supposed to represent grass and sky, even though the grass itself forms a wide elliptical band around the sky in the middle of the table.

If the table had been circular then the concentric circles of the background would have been easy to mosaic – one just works inwards towards a ruler nailed to the centre point (see the Underwater Panel on p84). In this case, however, I had concentric ellipses to deal with, which are much more difficult. As one travels inwards the proportion of the major to the minor axis changes and the ellipse keeps getting narrower, so I had to add 'banana' shapes at regular intervals to compensate and get back on the right track.

Together the foliage forms a sort of daisy chain, linking up the outer ring of the ellipse (see diagram, below).

The green lines on this diagram show how the animals themselves link up along the major axis of the table. The red line shows how the foliage elements link.

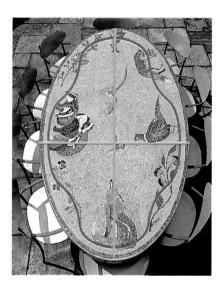

Nautilus Shell and Octopus Table

This was a very specific commission: to design, make and mosaic a large square table on a cylindrical base, with a nautilus shell on top and an octopus swimming around the cylinder. Cinca ceramic was the medium decided upon quite early on. I usually send samples of the tesserae to the client so that they can see for themselves the difference between the reflective glass and the non-reflective ceramic.

I like to involve the client in the design stage, but once I start mosaicing, I try and keep them away until the mosaic is finished. This is because any changes during the mosaicing process, however seemingly small they may appear, can involve days of extra work. The more people that have a say, the more likely it is that something won't be quite right. I am a firm believer in the adage that a camel is a horse designed by a committee. I once had a job that involved twenty-six letters to the client from me, which was very frustrating; I seemed to be spending more time composing letters than making the mosaic. Luckily, the mosaic was well-received in the end.

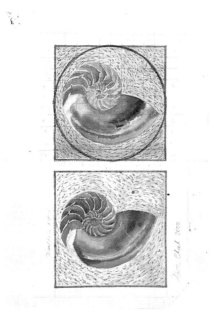

Nautilus Shell Artwork
Watercolour, 2000

It's a good idea to give the client a choice of designs, even if it's just a simple matter of deciding between two different colourways. The client then feels more involved and rightly thinks that he or she has had a say in the decision-making at the design stage.

This artwork shows two design variations, one of which has the shell contained within a circle to show how the design would look as a circular table.

Nautilus Shell Tabletop
129x129cm (51x51in), Cinca ceramic, 2000

I tried to persuade my client that this shell would look better within a circular tabletop as illustrated top left and below, but he was adamant about wanting a square format. This shell is a very realistic representation compared to the cartoony octopus on the column.

Octopus Artwork
Watercolour, 2000

These two octopuses are very similar in character, but I wanted to show two different colourways. I wanted to make sure that there wasn't a beginning and end to the octopus, so I interlaced the legs, as shown. If there had been a starting point, then I think it would have looked like a seam on the finished mosaic.

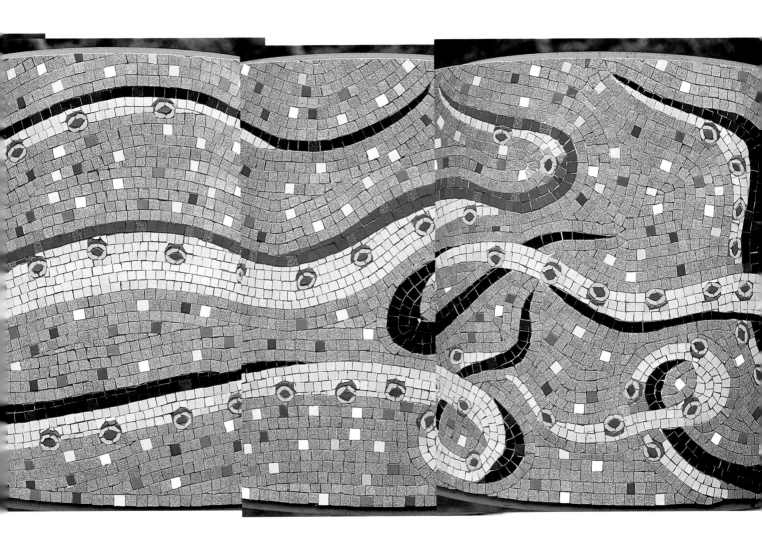

Octopus Base
48x61cm (19x24in), Cinca ceramic, 2000

It was important that the octopus's head wasn't too high up because it wouldn't have been seen beneath the large tabletop overhanging it.

The actual construction and making of the table base was tricky. We decided to construct it out of rings of MDF stacked on top of each other. My carpenter friend, Rex Hope, designed it with every sixth ring having a smaller internal diameter, so that we could run a length of studding through them. Once this studding was bolted in place, the tabletop located onto the bolts and twisted clockwise into a locked position. It was important that the top should be removable because the whole table was shipped to the other side of the world, where termites are probably eating it as I write.

Hare Table

IT IS NOT an exaggeration to say that the lady who commissioned this mosaic is mad about hares! Sculptures of trumpeting hares greet you as you arrive at the house and everywhere you look there is a hare looking back at you with those big, wild eyes. So it wasn't difficult to come up with the design for this tabletop.

The concentric circles used for the background, in this case sky, are always a gift when working on a circular mosaic. Having them 'crash' into the grass, which is sweeping from left to right, seems to emphasize the circularity, a bit like breaking rhythm in music. Achieving the sunset in the sky was not as easy as it looks, given the limited palette. I wanted to avoid solid 'bands' of colour and to filter through the pinks to the blue.

Hare Table
100cm (39¼in) diameter,
Cinca ceramic, 2000

The association of hares with the moon is a long
established one, usually depicted by star-gazing hares.
Mine is more like the nursery rhyme cow jumping over
the moon. The detail on the following pages shows
clearly how the *opus vermiculatum* around the hare
itself blends into the *andamento* of the whole piece
along its back and tummy.

Sculpture and objets d'art

I REALIZED QUITE early on in my mosaicing career that I wanted to push my mosaics beyond the boundaries of the 'picture' stage. I began to experiment with simple cut-out shapes, like the Emperor Angel Fish (see p47).

These cut-out shapes soon became more and more ambitious, getting larger and more elaborate, such as the Saint (see p126). I am currently working on a life-sized three-dimensional mosaiced cow for Cow Parade 2002 (see p120).

It's important to remember that the mosaic is only a 'skin' and if you think of it in these terms then you quickly realize that it is possible to mosaic literally anything. Remember, too, though, that the mosaic material has no structural strength in itself – being made up of lots of small parts – so a plastic plant pot is still going to be a plastic plant pot if you cover it with mosaic.

It's lovely to have the luxury to be able to work on these larger projects. Naturally, they can take a long time and it's always much longer than you first imagined. Whenever I have finished one of these large projects, I get an enormous sense of relief at being able to go back to making a manageable, simple, small piece. It reminds me of my time as an illustrator, when, having worked in colour for a while, I really enjoyed going back to straightforward black and white.

Leaping Frog
90x144cm (35x56in), smalti, vitreous glass, plain and coloured mirror, beach glass, stained glass and pebbles, 1999

See also p118.

I WANTED TO show the 'evolution' of a piece of my mosaic sculpture and this is the best example I have. A large, ambitious work such as this never happens overnight and often never happens at all, getting stuck at one of the stages shown here. The final stage of this one (see p116) is the direct result of an accident in firing one of my ceramic birds. A large sculptural mosaic like this represents a huge investment of my time, as well as the large financial investment of commissioning the blacksmith and the sheer cost of such a large quantity of mosaic materials.

Guinea Fowl Painting
40x30cm (16x2in), watercolour, 2000

This is really a drawing of the ceramic bird, below and not a real one. The reason that I wanted to include this drawing and the ceramic piece in this book is to give an example of how my mosaics can sometimes evolve. The large mosaic guinea fowl sculpture (see p116) would not have been realized without the ceramic work and drawings that came before it.

Guinea Fowl Slab Pot
16.5x18cm (6½x7in), stoneware ceramic, 2000

I remembered seeing guinea fowl in bird parks, but it quickly became apparent to me that if I was going to develop this theme in any meaningful way then I would need to get hold of some real ones of my own. I bought two black and two silver ones, both with elegant white dots.

Once I had the real birds in my own garden it became easier to study them from life. What struck me most was the elegant line of their backs. They reminded me of a society lady arriving at a premiere wearing a dress with a long train trailing behind her.

This piece is essentially a slab pot, made by wrapping a flat triangle of clay round on itself and then pinching a head on the top.

Guinea Fowl Mosaic (OPPOSITE)
30x39cm (11x15in), smalti, marble and Cinca ceramic, 2000

This is the first in this series of works which I made before I bought my own guinea fowl. The cloak depicted was from memory and rough drawings made in bird parks. In fact, the real birds don't look like this. I include this piece to show how one's memory plays tricks on you and can't be relied on when it comes to reproducing naturalistic detail.

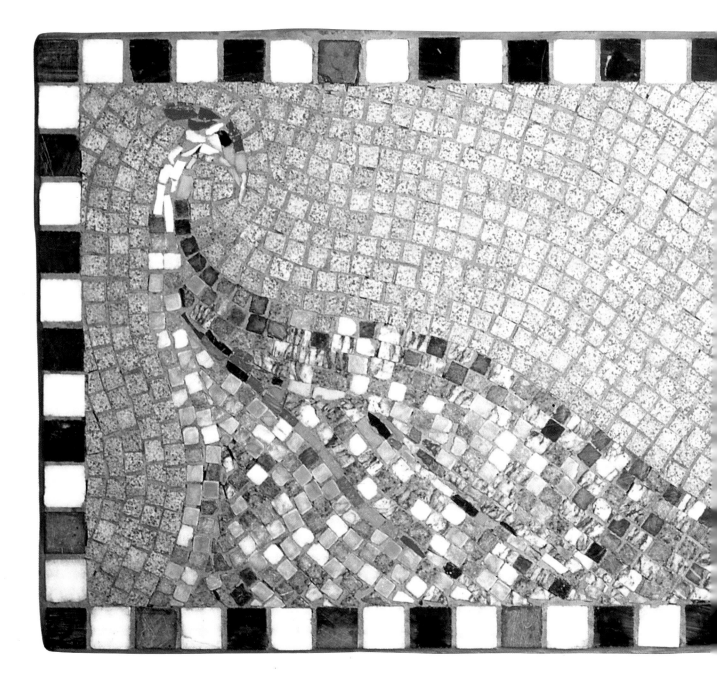

Guinea Fowl Mosaic
30x29cm (11x11in), smalti, marble and Cinca ceramic, 2000

This is a mosaic of the ceramic piece on p112. It was made indirect and because the marble used on the bird was so much chunkier than the ceramic background, the contrast seemed sufficient when I looked at it prior to casting it up. I wanted a subtle effect in order to stress the elegance that I was trying to achieve.

However when the slab was turned out of the mould and the underside of the ceramic and marble were flush, I was disappointed with how close in tone they were to each other.

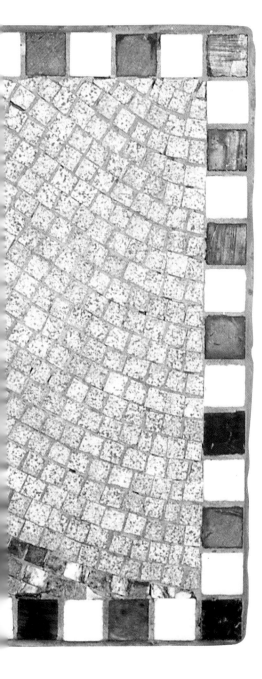

A Pair of Guinea Fowl Tiles
15x15cm (6x6in), raku-fired tiles, 2000

This pair are really an extension of the watercolour on p112. Painting on tiles makes you economize your line and be less fussy. I was able to reduce my guinea fowl down to a simple, flowing, triangular shape. This helped me enormously when it came to drawing out the template for the metal substructure of the sculpture on p116.

Guinea Fowl Mosaic
49x30cm (19x11in), smalti, marble and Cinca ceramic, 2000

I decided to have another go at making a guinea fowl mosaic, this time with the background a speckled green-grey, which would hopefully differentiate it from the bird. I think that this one is altogether more successful. In both this one and the mosaic opposite, I like the fact that the only smalti used are the few pieces that make up the head.

Guinea Fowl Mosaic Sculpture
(FOLLOWING PAGES)
102x66cm (40x26in), smalti, marble and stoneware-fired ceramic head, 2000

I made lots of ceramic slab pot guinea fowl like the one on p112, experimenting with different ways of capturing the white spots. Sometimes I scraffitoed through a black slip to reveal white clay and sometimes I 'plugged' the body with white clay spots.

One such piece split in two in the kiln, but the 'S' shape that remained was still able to stand up. This gave me the idea of making one in metal, simply by bending a single sheet of steel and adding a sculpted head, thus proving that even a disaster can become an inspiration for your next mosaic. Blacksmith, Julian Coode was able to do the metalwork for me and we decided to use marble to depict the spots against a smalti body.

The head was sculpted and fired to stoneware temperature, so that it can withstand the cold British climate. I like this piece and think that in works particularly well in my garden with the real guinea fowl scratching about nearby.

Leaping Frog
90×144cm (35×56in), smalti, vitreous glass, plain and coloured mirror, beach glass, stained glass and pebbles, 1999

By 'beach glass' I mean glass such as broken bottles that have been left on the beach and worn down by the tide over a period of time. It has a lovely opaque quality, reminiscent of precious stones.

I drew the silhouette of the frog and the water onto a sheet of steel plate and then my friendly blacksmith Julian Coode cut it out for me with an oxy-acetylene torch. The tesserae were stuck to the metal with a special epoxy glue that is suitable for use underwater. The large pieces of mirror were stuck as close to each other as possible and then the gaps filled in with smaller and smaller tesserae, finishing off with nibbled vitreous glass.

The frog is mosaiced on both sides. When I mosaiced the second side, I hung the frog over a table and placed a mirror below it; I simply had to reproduce the reflected image.

I've made lots of pieces like this, suitable for use in ponds and rivers. They always look terribly solid and heavy on dry land, but as soon as they are placed in water, with the water reflected in the mirror and visible through the cut holes in the steel, the solidity is broken up and the frog or fish really seems to fly through the air.

Cheeky Cow

224x112x112cm (88x44x44in), fibreglass cow, vitreous glass and acrylic paint, 2001

This mosaic is a work in progress; it's taking an age to finish. As a guide, I can tell you that each patchwork square takes about two hours to mosaic properly – it's never as easy as it looks. So, the deadline for this book has come around before I've managed to complete the cow. However, I wanted to include it in these pages as it shows the way in which my work is progressing and what I am trying to aspire to.

This cow is one of 500 that are currently being painted or decorated by artists throughout Britain. When they are finished they will be put on show in public places around London. After a few weeks they will be auctioned off for Childline, the children's charity.

Cheeky Cow Detail (RIGHT)

Mine is really a bovine version of the Harlequin (see p18). I thought that he had worked well and wanted to stick with the same palette for this three-dimensional version. When I started, I cut out a few diamonds of different sizes to see which one worked best. I thought that it would then be a simple case of drawing round this chosen template to create the patchwork harlequin suit. How wrong I was! The undulating form of the cow meant that the lines had to be manipulated a great deal in order to follow its muscular body. As always, you go with what looks right visually and not what is mathematically correct. Well, so far so good; I'll let you know how she finally works out in my next book.

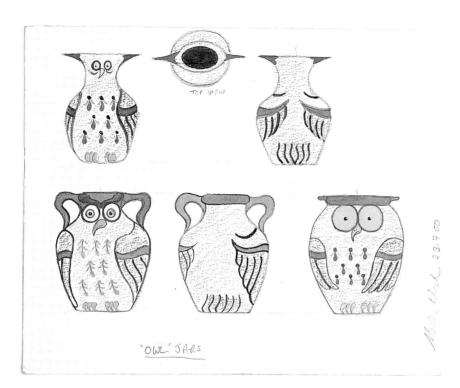

Owl Jar Artwork

30×20cm (12×8in), watercolour and crayon, 2000

Before making coil pots in clay, I sometimes play with various possibilities on paper first. I drew these designs while I was on holiday in Greece and unable to do any mosaic or ceramic work. Planning future projects for when I get home helps to compensate for missing the feel of getting clay on my hands, which as any potter will tell you, becomes an addiction.

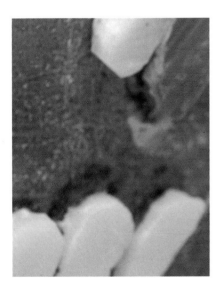

Mosaic Details

The mosaic in this case was a bit of an after thought; I felt that the jug would benefit from the addition of some bright colour. The mosaic was simply stuck onto the pot with PVA and then grouted. But then this gave me an idea that came to fruition in the Eagle Jug (see p125).

Owl Jar

20×24cm (8×9in), clay, copper carbonate and vitreous glass, 2001

Among my favourite artists is Robert Wallace Martin, who made most of his salt-glazed 'Wally Birds' between 1885-1904. I love their rook-like quality. His owls though, are truer to nature. The Fitzwilliam Museum in Cambridge boasts a wonderful owl modelled by Wallace Martin in 1903. Standing at 103cm (40in) high, it is the largest known and it really is a masterpiece.

I must admit that this ceramic coiled pot is an unashamed homage to Wallace Martin, whose imagination gave rise to a whole procession of grotesque and humourous creatures masquerading as jugs, spoon-warmers, vases and toast racks. Anyone familiar with my work will see instantly why his birds appeal to me so much.

Palm Pot (OPPOSITE)
28×35cm (11×13in), clay, copper carbonate and
vitreous glass, 2001

This pot is inspired by a Kamares-style pot in
the Herakleion Museum, Crete. I remember the
day that I was wandering round the museum
staring at the various artefacts; this pot seemed
to be shouting at me from across the other side
of the room. You know that feeling, usually
experienced with music, when the hairs on the
back of your neck suddenly stand on end:
occasionally that can happen when you see a
great work of art. You don't need to be told
that it's special – you instinctively know it is.

I suppose that one should leave such things
alone – given that there's no way in which you
could improve on the original. But that 'I've got
to have it' feeling was overwhelming and clearly
the only way I was ever going to get even close
to getting my hands on anything remotely similar
was to make one for myself.

The pot was coiled from clay and left to go
leather hard. Vitreous glass mosaic is 3mm (⅛in)
thick, so allowing extra depth for the adhesive,
the pot had to be made quite thick. The areas
where the black mosaic was to go could then
be carved back with a metal tool. When it was
completely dry, I bisque-fired the pot and then
re-fired it with a hint of copper scrubbed into
the body to make it look old and weathered.

Finally, the pot was mosaiced with the three
different blacks available in vitreous glass; the
main one was the 'grainy' black, but I felt that it
needed peppering with the shiny black and the
veined black to add some texture. I thought that
opus regulatum was the only choice here: the
resulting effect of the addition of the mosaic
needed to be one of calm, not movement. It
would be interesting to see what date an
archaeologist would suggest for the origination
of my pot!

Eagle Jug
23×37cm (9×14in), clay, copper carbonate and vitreous glass, 2001

For this jug I anticipated the addition of the mosaic and carved out the
relevant areas when the clay was leather hard, prior to bisque firing. The
result, not surprisingly, is more considered than the Owl Jar, (see p123).
Note those owls again, this time drawn into the clay with a tool. Nothing is
entirely new, as is usually the case with my work, and you probably won't
be surprised to learn that the inspiration behind this piece was a jug, dating
from 1400BC, in the Archaeological Museum in Athens.

Ordelaffo Falier (OPPOSITE)
54x180cm (21x71in), coloured and gold leaf smalti and raku-fired pieces, 1998

This saint is inspired by a detail from the *Pala D'Oro*, an enamelled screen altarpiece in St Mark's, Venice. I suppose it shows the contrary nature of my personality that when confronted by six centuries of the greatest mosaics ever produced, I should draw inspiration from the one thing in the building that's not a mosaic!

The original figure was only a few centimetres tall, but I wanted to make mine life-size. I could, of course, have mosaiced the face and hands, but I felt that by making them as *opus sectile* inserts, I was able to capture the delicacy of the original figure. The upside-down white hearts were incorporated in the mosaicing of the cloak at random, but the green clover tiles used to make up the floor had to be carefully numbered and individually cut to fit together.

I was lucky enough to visit the famous Orsoni smalti factory while in Venice. I purchased a huge bag of gold leaf smalti there, which meant that I could afford to use so much of it in this piece. Normally the sheer cost of this material, if bought in the UK, would have made it prohibitively expensive to use on this scale.

At first glance the mosaic looks fairly symmetrical, but on closer inspection one discovers that it is the very lack of symmetry – the way that the Saint's right leg is sticking out – that gives the piece its commanding presence.

St Augustine's Abbey Mosaic Triptych
Each panel 39x126cm (15x49in), vitreous glass, smalti, glazed tiles and ceramic pieces, 2000

This triptych showing the monk, St Augustine, was commissioned by English Heritage as a community project with local school children for St Augustine's Abbey in Canterbury. I started off by visiting the schools and talking about monastic life with the children. Initially all of their drawings focused totally on the monk praying and it was with some difficulty that I was able to convince the children that monks did other things apart from just praying all day! Gardening, brewing, eating and drinking, washing and bee-keeping all eventually featured in the finished mosaic.

PART FOUR

Practicalities

The Budd technique

THIS TECHNIQUE WAS developed by Kenneth Budd in the 1950s and is still used by Kenneth's son, Oliver Budd, one of our greatest contemporary mosaic artists. The technique involves fitting an indirect mosaic into an aluminium tray. This means that the tray can be taken off the wall and relocated if you move house. The tray can be bought from a metal fabricator (see Suppliers or your local phone book). Because aluminium oxidises, the tray needs to be powder coated (see Suppliers or ask your fabricator to do this for you).

The adhesive used is called 'Bal Flex' (see Suppliers), a two-part rubber adhesive. One part is liquid latex and the other is a powder containing latex and cement. The ratio is 3 pts powder: 2 pts liquid. This is simple if you use the entire contents of both containers (7.5 kg powder: 5 ltr liquid) but if you require less this works out as 1.5 kg of powder: 1 ltr liquid This is not as tricky as it sounds if you use imperial weights, as it converts to 50 oz: 1¾ pt, or 5 oz: 3½ fl oz.

Amazingly this adhesive never goes completely hard, but remains flexible. This is excellent with metal trays, as the metal can be a light one such as aluminium and the mosaic will simply flex with the metal.

The minimum depth of tray my fabricator was able to supply was 10mm (½in). The thickness of the vitreous glass tiles is 3mm (⅛in) so I inserted a 5mm (½in) metal lath (available from builders merchants) between the tray and the mosaic. The lath is flattened as much as possible and then held down in the tray with regularly spaced weights.

Sealife Panel Artwork
100x100cm (39x39in), charcoal and pastel on craft paper, 2000

I loved making the fish panel on p23 so I decided to make a companion piece for myself. I love to inject as much humour as possible into my mosaics and I think of this piece as the humorous version of the original mosaic. This is the full-size artwork from which I made the mosaic.

Sealife Panel

100x100cm (39x39in), vitreous glass, 2000

Compositionally this mosaic owes a lot to the previous fish panel, relying on strong diagonals to hold it together. The shells are placed simply to help the overall flow made by the vigorous fish. Use of *opus regulatum* for the background is essential here in order to calm down the overall feel of this lively piece.

The squid is a cephalopod, which literally means 'head-footed' and refers to the way in which the arms and tentacles of the creatures sprout directly from their heads. It was a bad day when I learnt that a squid has ten legs and not eight like an octopus, as I had supposed!

1 The lath is stuck down with 'Gripfill', a very strong bonding agent applied with an injection gun. This takes at least a day to set.

2 The next day, mix up the 'Bal flex' as instructed on the packet (add the powder to the liquid) and, using a grout spreader, firstly fill in the gaps between the mesh of the lath.

3 Next, smooth on an even 2-mm (⅛in-) thick bed of adhesive. Comb the adhesive in one direction only to avoid creating any air pockets. Place the completed indirect mosaic face up onto the bed of adhesive. It is a good idea to place a board on top of the mosaic to help flatten it. Weight this down if you think it is necessary.

4 The next day moisten the paper with cold water, let it soak in for a few minutes and then peel it off.

I find that if you pull the paper back onto itself at 180°, as opposed to 90°, then the risk of pulling away any tesserae is reduced. Take your time over removing the paper and if any tesserae come loose, stick them back down again with freshly mixed adhesive.

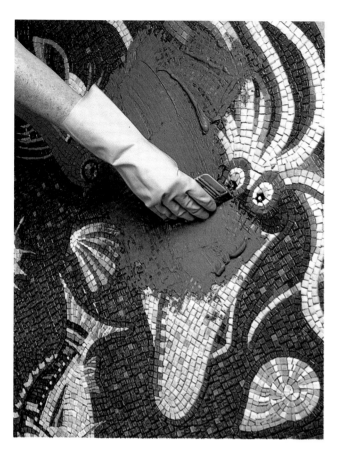

5 The next day, grout the mosaic as usual.

6 Before fixing the finished mosaic to the wall, remove five tesserae – one from each corner and one from the middle. Gently prise the tesserae out with a metal tool, then scrape out the adhesive below them. Drill a hole through the metal where the tesserae were. These are the location points for the screws.

7 Using a wax crayon and thin paper, make a rubbing of the corners and the centre of the mosaic, indicating which is the missing tesserae in each case by circling it. Keep these rubbings in a safe place so that when you want to take the mosaic down, you can identify which tesserae are hiding the screws.

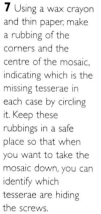

8 Offer the mosaic up to the wall and position it as desired, with a spirit level on the top to ensure that it is horizontal. Using a pencil, mark the screw position on the wall through the top two holes. Remove the mosaic and drill the holes, then insert the appropriate wall plugs. Temporarily hang the mosaic on the wall from these two holes and then mark the other three screw positions. Remove the mosaic, drill and plug the remaining three holes. Re-hang the mosaic. Replace the five missing tesserae, sticking them down with fresh adhesive, and grout them in place.

Working to commission

The clients

I FIND THAT clients can vary enormously, from the perfect to the impossible. It is important to do enough preliminary work to be able to seal the job with the client, but don't take the designs too far, as this restricts your flexibility. Also there is a financial consideration: how long can you afford to spend on a speculative proposition if you haven't yet clinched the job? Are there any other artists pitching for the same job?

Commissions differ from straight sales (someone buying a pre-made mosaic 'off the peg'), as there will be a relationship between you, the client and the mosaic. The client obviously thinks that it is his or her mosaic, but because it is your work you think that it is your mosaic! The truth of course, is that you are both correct.

Choosing the right artist is just as important with mosaic as it is with any other medium, such as portraiture. While no one in their right mind would commission a portrait by simply looking up 'portrait painters' in the phone book, people often do exactly that when trying to hunt down a mosaic artist. If a client was desperate for a mosaic of a boat or a steam locomotive, for example, then I would be the wrong artist and I would try and point them towards another artist whose work would suit them better.

If you have been a professional artist for some time, then hopefully the client will trust your judgement and opinion. This is where a portfolio comes into its own. Hopefully the work will speak for itself in showing the sort of subject matter that you like to work on. I have had clients who did not want to know anything about the work: 'Surprise me!', was the only guide I had for the Wildlife Table (see p90). Other clients want total control of every stage of the creative process.

The price

Usually the initial enquiry for a mosaic commission is by phone or email. Money rears its ugly head almost immediately and even after all these years, I still find it the hardest thing to deal with and to explain to the prospective client.

The fact is that detailed, 'nibbled' mosaic work can take four or five times longer to do than background work, so if there is a lot of background in the mosaic you can charge less. It helps to have a rate for nibbled work and a separate lower rate for background work, so that you can give a fair price. But obviously you can't price the job up in these terms until you have designed it – a chicken and egg situation.

My solution to this is to have a blanket price per square metre, which includes design, delivery and installation. Many artists prefer to add these items on to the price of the actual mosaic, because it looks so much less if itemised. My friend

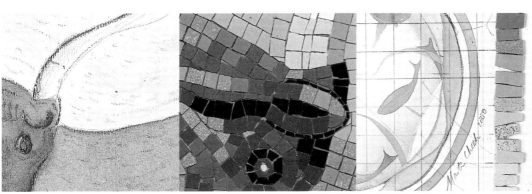

Oliver Budd charges ten per cent of the total budget for a design fee, which is a good idea, especially if you have to keep redesigning the piece, because you can keep invoicing for the extra work.

The portfolio

Your portfolio is the single most important thing when it comes to getting you work. If you want to build up your portfolio by adding to existing commissions, my advice is to look at the 'holes' in your existing range of work.

Do you have mosaics made in lots of different media: vitreous glass, ceramic, smalti, marble, tiles, etc? If you do not already have a piece in smalti, it is unlikely that a client will risk spending such a lot of money on a mosaic when they are not sure what the final result will look like. Is your subject matter varied enough? Do you have mosaics of birds, animals, people, landscapes, abstract work, patterns, borders, etc? Again, if you only have abstract work to show then you are unlikely to get a commission to mosaic an animal.

Obviously you have to choose what you want to mosaic and make your portfolio reflect your own personal taste. I find, however, that clients like to see evidence of what they are asking for in your existing work. I once failed to get a commission because the client wanted a gold finish and there wasn't anything gold in my portfolio at the time. Needless to say, I rectified this soon afterwards and this issue hasn't arisen since.

Some clients lack the imagination to see that you are capable of producing a mosaic of anything that they can think of. My response to this is to try and block all the exits by having appropriate samples in my portfolio, thus giving them no excuses not to commission me.

The photographs

It goes without saying that keeping a record of your work is absolutely essential in order to add to your portfolio. That said, one is usually so pleased to have finished a piece of work, and so desperate to deliver it and get paid, that the photography takes a back step and sometimes gets overlooked.

I find mosaics difficult to photograph. While you want to show the play of light on the tiles, too much shine on the surface will make it glare and not enough will make the work look flat. If you know a friend who is good at taking photographs, then try and persuade them to do it for you. If not, a decent single lens reflex (SLR) camera is essential. Bracket the shots, by taking seven pictures at different exposures, with the one you think is correct as the middle one, then you can choose the best result.

Most galleries and directories ask for transparencies, but don't rely on getting these returned – either take lots of slides of the same mosaic or get copies made and keep the original.

Where to see mosaics

THERE ARE MOSAICS all over the world. They date from ancient times to the present and can be seen on floors and walls in buildings, museums, galleries, archaeological sites, churches, mosques, underground stations and subways. It is always a delight and a surprise to stumble on them in the most unexpected places. The list of where to see mosaics is as varied as it is endless, so here are a few of the better known ones.

Algeria

Timgad; 2nd century.

Austria

Vienna; Oesterreichisches Museum; 'Waiting' and 'Embrace' by Gustav Klimt; 1905-1909.

Czech Republic

Prague; St Vitus's Cathedral; 14th century.

Cyprus

Kiti; Church of Angeloktistou; 5th century.

Kourion; House of Eustolios, building of the Achilles mosaic; 4th century BC to 4th century AD.

Paphos; 4th century BC to 4th century AD.

Egypt

Alexandria; Graeco-Roman Museum.

Mt Sinai; Monastery of St Catherine; 6th century.

France

Biot, Alpes-Maritimes; Musée de Ferdnand Léger; 1954.

Hauterives; Le Palais Idéal du Facteur Cheval; 1879-1912.

Nice; University of Nice; 'Faculty of Law' mosaic by Lino Melano, from a cartoon by Marc Chagall; 1967.

Nice; Chagall Museum; 'Zodiac' by Marc Chagall; 20th century.

Paris; The Louvre; ancient, Roman.

Paris; St Genevive sous Bois; Tomb of Nureyev; 1980s.

Paris; UNESCO House; by Jean Bazaine; 1958.

Germany

Frankfurt am Main; Dresdner Bank; by Heinz Mack; 1980s.

Hamburg; Sankt Nikolai; by Oskar Kokoscha; 20th century.

Nennig; Saabruchen; 2nd-4th centuries.

Trier; Rheinisiches Landesmuseum.

Greece

Delos; Greek island in the Cyclades; 2nd century BC.

Nea Moni; Chios; 11th century.

Pella; Macedonia; Pebble Mosaics; 4th century BC.

Thessaloniki; Churches of St George and Hosios David; 5th century.

Thessaloniki; Church of St Sophia; 11th century.

Italy

Aquileia; Basilica and Museum of Archaeology; 1st century BC to 3rd century AD.

Herculaneum; 1st century.

Milan; Chapel of S. Aquilano; 4th century.

Ostia Antica; 3rd-2nd century BC.

Ravenna; Church of San Vitale; 6th century.

Ravenna; Mausoleum of Galla Placidia; 5th century.

Ravenna; Nation Museum.

Ravenna; Parco della Pace; 1980s.

Ravenna; St Apollinare in Classe; 6th century.

Rome; S. Clemente; 12th century.

Rome; S. Prassede; 9th century.

Sicily; Cathedral of Monreale; 12th century.

Venice; Cathedral of St Marco; 11th-15th centuries.

Venice; Island of Murano, the basilica of SS. Maria e Donato; 12th century.

Jordon

Jerash; Archaeological Museum and sites; 2nd-7th centuries.

Madaba; Archaeological Museum and sites; 5th-8th centuries.

Mount Nebo; Museum and sites; 5th-8th centuries.

Israel / Palestine

Beth Alpha; Synagogue; 6th century.

Gaza; Synagogue; 6th century.

Hammath Tiberius; 6th century.

Jericho; Khirbet-el-Mafjar; 8th century.

Jerusalem; Dome of the Rock mosque; 7th century.

Lebanon

Beirut; Beit el Din palace; 6th century.

Libya

Zliten; Roman Villa; 2nd century.

Mexico

Mexico City; University, Faculty of Medicine; by Eppens; 20th century.

Mexico City; University, Rectorado Building; Mosaic bas-relief by David Alfaro; 20th century.

Mexico City; University Library; by Juan O'Gorman; 20th century.

Morocco

Moulay Idris; site of Volubilis; 2nd century.

Portugal

Conimbrega; near Coimbra; 3rd century.

Russia

St Petersburg; Cathedral of St Isaac; 19th century.

Kiev; S. Sophia; 11th century.

Spain

Ampurias; 1st-3rd centuries.

Barcelona; Sagrada Familia Church and Parc Guell; by Antonio Gaudi; early 20th century.

Cordoba; Andalusia; Mihrab in the Mosque; 10th century.

Sweden

Stockholm; City Hall; Einah Forseth; 1920s.

Syria

Damascus; The Great Mosque; 8th century.

Turkey

Antioch; (capital of Roman Syria) Villa of Constantine; 2nd century.

Istanbul; The Great Palace; 6th century.

Istanbul; Haghia Sophia; 6th-12th centuries.

Kariye; Chora Museum; 11th-14th centuries.

Tunisia

El Djem; Archaeological Museum and sites; 2nd century.

Tunis; The Bardo Museum; 2nd-6th centuries.

UK

Birmingham; 'The Great Western Railway' and 'The Kennedy Memorial' by Kenneth Budd; 1950s.

Cranbrook; Wealds Sports Centre; 'Aquaflight' by Oliver Budd; 2000.

Fishbourne; Roman Palace; 1st-3rd centuries.

Kingston-upon-Hull; City Museum; 4th century.

Leeds; Church of St Aidan's; by Frank Brangwen; 1914-16

London; Albert Memorial, Kensington Gore; Italian-made Victorian mosaic recently restored by Trevor Caley; 1860s.

London; Army Museum; 'Peace' by Martin Cheek; 1994.

London; The British Museum, Holborn; Roman, Mexican and ancient mosaics.

London; The Gilbert Collection; micro-mosaics; 17th-early 20th centuries.

London; The National Gallery, Trafalgar Square; 'Professions and Leisure' by Boris Anrep; 1928-1952.

London; St Benedict's Church, Pimlico Road; Italian-made Victorian mosaic.

London; St Paul's Cathedral; 1870-1920s.

London; The Tate Britain, Pimlico; William Blake Room by Boris Anrep; 1950s.

London; Tottenham Court Road Underground; by Eduardo Paolozzi; 1970s.

London; Westminster Cathedral, Victoria; early-mid 20th century.

Newport; 'The Chartist Mosaic' by Kenneth Budd; 1977; 'The Florist Mosaic' by Kenneth and Oliver Budd; 1992.

Somerset; Taunton Museum; 4th century.

Wigan; Judas's Church; by Hans Unger and Eberhard Schulze; 1965.

Wilton; Wiltshire, Church of St Mary and St Nicolas; 19th century.

Wales; Machynlleth, Museum of Modern Art; 'Taliesin Mosaic' and 'Machynlleth Mela' by Martin Cheek; 1996.

USA

San Diego; Horton Plaza; 20th century.

Chicago; 'Four Seasons'; designed by Marc Chagall.

New York; Third Street; abstract mosaic by Hans Hoffman; 20th century.

New York; William O'Grady School, Coney Island; designed by Ben Shahn; 20th century.

Glossary of mosaic terms

Andamento

The generic word to describe the general 'flow' of the mosaic. eg: The *andamento* of the Harlequin mosaic (see p18) is circular.

Direct method

The most basic and common technique for making mosaics. Tesserae are cut and stuck, face up, directly on to the base. The surfaces of mosaics made using this technique are, therefore, not always smooth and much licence can be taken with the shape and texture of the tesserae.

Indirect method

A mosaic technique often used for making large-scale work intended for outdoor settings. Tesserae are stuck face down on to paper with a temporary, water-based bonding agent, generally gum arabic or wallpaper paste. The mosaic can then be transported, whole or in sections, and set in its permanent base with the paper side uppermost. The paper is then peeled away to reveal the finished work, which can then be grouted. The resulting surface is usually smooth.

Interstices

The gaps between the rows of tesserae create flow lines, or interstices. It is the interstices that in turn create the *andamento*.

Opus musivum

If the *opus vermiculatum* is continued outwards to fill a larger area then this area becomes *opus musivum*. This is the most rhythmic and lyrical of all the opus techniques: literally it means 'pertaining to the muses'.

Opus regulatum

A Roman mosaic technique whereby regular, square tesserrae are applied in straight rows. The result is a brick-wall pattern and is frequently used to fill large expanses of background.

Opus sectile

When a part of the mosaic, such as a head, consists of only one section, this part is known as *opus sectile*. If the whole area of the mosaic is covered in this way, then the resulting effect is more like stained glass or marquetry.

Opus tessellatum

A Roman mosaic technique whereby regular, square tesserae are applied in a rectilinear arrangement. The resulting uniform grid design is most frequently used to fill large expanses of background. You would expect this to be the most common *opus* for background work, but in fact, because the tesserae are irregular, the rows rarely meet up on two axes. Therefore *opus regulatum* is the most common *opus* for background work.

Opus vermiculatum

A Roman mosaic technique whereby regular, square tesserrae are applied in a row around the main mosaic motif to create a halo effect and emphasize the setting lines of the design. *Vermis* is the Latin word for 'worm' (eg: vermicelli), so you can think of this as the worm of tesserae that outlines the main figure.

Tesserae

A Roman word meaning 'cube'. These cubes are the basic building blocks of mosaic. The term now embraces diverse materials, including marble, ceramic, glass, broken crockery, mirror glass, stones and pebbles.

Mosaic materials

Ceramic

All types of ceramic can of course be broken up and incorporated into a mosaic. It's very useful though to be able to buy sheets of ceramic tiles in various colours and to know that you won't run out of any particular colour. Cinca is the brand name of one such type of unglazed ceramic tile made in Portugal, but available in sheets in this country. Cinca comes in sheets of 14x14 tiles, each square measuring 23x23mm (1x1in).

Because they are so much heavier than vitreous glass, the glue binding them to the backing paper is stronger and takes longer to soak off. Even then, the tiles have a tendency to stick together while drying, so it is advisable to spread them out individually on the towel so that they don't touch each other.

The colour range is good – there are usually 25 different colours to choose from. The main difference between vitreous glass and Cinca ceramic is that vitreous is made of glass and is therefore shiny and reflective, whereas Cinca is an un-glazed and non-reflective ceramic. This can be used to good effect by placing an area of one next to the other: the vitreous will appear to come forward while the Cinca will appear to recede. Therefore a Cinca-mosaiced background floor will allow a vitreous or smalti subject to stand out.

Cinca tiles don't have a 'right' and 'wrong' side, which means that you have the added advantage of being able to flip them over if you wish. As you work, you will appreciate how advantageous this is when you have a piece the right shape, but the wrong way round.

If the mosaic is made entirely of Cinca, then the effect will be a calm one, reminiscent of Indian art. Cinca is excellent for floor mosaics as the tiles are completely flat and, if set into a solid floor, can withstand a person walking across them.

Found Objects

Roman mosaics were made of natural stone cut up into small cubes. Natural stone and marble are still used extensively in mosaics throughout the world. It is also possible to use found objects, such as beads, buttons and shells – in fact anything that can be combined with anything else to make a cohesive whole.

Anyone who has ever played with pebbles on the beach will immediately recognise the attraction of pebble mosaics. The Alhambra in Granada, Spain, is one of the most impressive places to see pebble mosaics. What surprises most people is the fact that the amount of pebble visible above the cement is only the tip of the iceberg. The pebbles can be inserted straight into a bed of wet sand and cement, but if you intend to walk on your finished pebble mosaic it is worth making a simple mould and laying the pebbles indirect (upside down) into a bed of sand. The thickness of the sand bed will form the 'rebate', determining the amount of pebble visible above the layer of concrete.

It's horrifying to see broken bottles on the beach. However, glass worn down by the motion of the sea is very pleasing and a treasure to any self-respecting mosaic artist.

Broken crockery is a wonderful material for mosaic. Some mosaic artists have made this medium their own. I don't think it's as simple as it looks: to create a piece that really works requires a good sense of colour and a good eye for basic design.

Smalti

This is the Roman word for 'melt'. Smalti is hand-made in Venice and until recently there were only three families still making it. The recipes and techniques have been kept secret and were handed from father to son down the generations.

Glass is melted in a cauldron and then poured out onto a metal sheet, where it is pressed down like a pizza. This glass pizza is then sawn up into little briquettes, measuring about 2×1 cm (¾×½in). It is supposed to be used with the smooth side down, thus emphasising its rippled top surface. Tiny air bubbles are sometimes visible; this is not a mistake but part of its intrinsic quality.

Smalti can be bought in a 20kg (44lb) 'irregular mix' box in much the same way as vitreous glass. In among the mix you will find tesserae that have a curved edge – these are the edges of the glass pizza. Although purists would argue that these shouldn't be used, I find them invaluable for such things as geckos' toes, where rounded edges are a great help.

Roman mosaics, although made mainly of natural stones, do sometimes contain the odd bit of smalti – usually bright colours like orange or blue – but it was really the Byzantines that made the material their own, creating entire frescoes out of it. Needless to say, being handmade, smalti is very expensive. Despite the price, it makes a lovely addition to any mosaic and can be used in small quantities.

Because of its uneven surface you do not need to grout smalti when working direct. The theory is that it 'self grouts': as you push the smalti into the tile adhesive, the adhesive is forced up between the gaps in the smalti.

It is no problem using smalti indirect, even if you want to combine it with other materials. Although it has a different thickness to vitreous glass, this does not matter as the top surface will always be flat.

Vitreous Glass

Vitreous simply means 'non-porous'. This is the material that is used to clad swimming pools. The colour range is good; the standard range consists of 50 colours and extra colours become available from time to time (snap these up whenever you see them). Naturally, because the majority of the market is swimming pools, there is a better choice of blues, greens and whites than of any other colour.

When you first see the colour chart, the number of colours available to the mosaic artist will no doubt impress you, but beware! Unlike paints you can't 'mix' these colours, you have to achieve the effect of 'mixing' by placing the different colours next to each other – like the pointillism achieved by Seurat. Once you have made a few mosaics, you too will be willing to kill for a subtle flesh colour, instead of having to choose between a soft, pastel pink and a flaming, fiery red.

Vitreous glass comes in sheets of 15x15 tiles, each square measuring 2x2cm (¾x¾in). Each coloured sheet has a series number, rather like oil paints. Not surprisingly, the very pale colours are the cheapest (Series 1) and the brightest colours, with metallic veining, are the most expensive (Series 4). For chemical reasons, namely because it contains gold, 'Candy Pink' has a series (Series 5) of its own.

When making mosaic art, the paper is soaked off by placing the sheet of tiles in a basin of hot water. After a few minutes the paper will float off. Remove the paper and rinse the tiles in more hot water. Throw them into a colander and spread them out onto an old dry towel. Remember to place each colour on its own towel – if you chuck the whole lot onto one towel you only have to sort them all out later.

Each colour can then be put in its own jar and the end result is a studio that looks more like a sweet shop than an artist's studio! When I replenish my mosaic jars before each course, the entire studio resembles a multi coloured laundry, with tiles of all colours of the rainbow spread across the floor on their own separate towels.

Alternatively, vitreous glass can be purchased as loose tiles in large 25kg (55lb) boxes, sold as mixed 'scrap' for about one third of the price of the sheets of tiles. There is nothing wrong with these loose tiles and they are soon sorted out into different jars. Because, as we have already said, vitreous glass is used mainly for swimming pools, you will get a predominance of blues, greens and whites, but you can, of course, top up any extra colours you require. It is a good idea to always have a mixed box around as they often contain colours that are not widely available or are from a different batch to the one you have bought, in which case the tiles may be a slightly different shade of the same colour.

Mosaic suppliers

UK

Martin Cheek Mosaic Kits
Flint House, 21 Harbour Street,
Broadstairs, Kent, CT10 1ET
Tel: 01843 861958
Website: www.martincheek.com
Email: martin@martincheek.com

Supplier of mixed bags of vitreous glass,
gold leaf smalti, Cinca ceramic, coloured
smalti and glazed ceramic tesserae and
a range of mosaic kits designed by
Martin Cheek.

Oliver Budd
Oliver Budd's Mosaic Studio, Unit 5A,
Crown Yard, Bedgebury Estate, Goudhurst,
Kent, TN17 2QZ
Tel: 01580 212643

Supplier of vitreous glass, marble. Will
cut to order and provide small marble
tesserae.

DW & G Heath (Croyden) Ltd
19 Portley Wood Road, Whyteleafe,
Surrey, CR3 0BQ
Tel: 020 8657 6349/01883 652546

Large stockist of mosaic tools and
materials: vitreous glass, smalti, glazed and
unglazed ceramic tesserae.

Edgar Udny & Co. Ltd
314 Balham High Road, London, SW17
Tel: 020 8767 8181

The UK's largest stockist of mosaic tools
and materials: vitreous glass, smalti, glazed
and unglazed ceramic tesserae.

Reed Harris Ltd
Riverside House, 27 Carnworth Road,
London, SW6 3HR
Tel: 020 7736 7511

Marble and ceramic tiles. Unglazed Cinca
tiles from Portugal. Full range of Ardex
materials.

The Mosaic Workshop
Tel/Fax: 020 7263 2997

Supplier of marble. Will cut to order and
provide small marble tesserae.

Other suppliers that may be of interest

United Tiles
Tel: 01622 757161

Suppliers of Bal flex, Fast flex, Ardipox PC
Wall Adhesive, Ardex X7.
Bisque fired tiles, ask for the thickest
available (6mm/$\frac{1}{4}$in) if you are going to
raku fire them.

Julian Coode
Nailbourne Forge, Court Hill, Littlebourne,
Canterbury, CT3 1TX
Tel: 01227 728336

Blacksmith.

SJL Fabrications
Wingham Industrial Estate, Goodnestone
Road, Wingham, Kent CT3 1AR
Tel: 01227 720886

Metal fabricators.

Windridge Coatings
Dane Valley Road, St Peters, Kent
Tel: 01843 604474

Powder coating.

Langley London Ltd
The Tile Centre, 161-167 Borough High
Street, London SE1 1HU
Tel: 020 7407 4444

Suppliers of vitreous glass and ceramic tiles.

Tower Ceramics
91 Parkway, Camden Town, London,
NW1 9PP
Tel: 020 7485 7192

Suppliers of fibreglass netting for
mosaicing onto.

USA

American Mosaic Co
912 First Street NW, Washington, DC
20001, USA

Arizona Art Supply
3236 N. 3rd Street, Phoenix, Arizona
85012, USA
Tel: (602) 264 9514

Berkshire Chemicals Inc
155 East 44th Street, New York, NY
10017, USA

Champions Craft
9750 Regency Square Blvd. Jacksonville,
Florida 32225 USA
Tel: (904) 725 3020

Costante Cravato
Tel: (914) 237 6210 or (305) 480 9028

Ed Hoys
16620 Frontenac Rd, Naperville,
Illinois 600563, USA
Tel: (800) 323 5668

Gager's Handicraft
1024 Nicollet Avenue, Minneapolis,
Minnesota 55403, USA

Mosaic Crafts Inc
80 West Street (Nr 6th Avenue),
New York, NY 10012, USA

Mosaic Mercantile
215 E. Louis 303, P.O.Box 1550, Livingston,
Montana 59047 USA

Mountaintop Mosaics
Sven Warner, P.O.Box 653, Castleton,
Vermont 05735, USA
T: (800) 564 4980
www.mountaintopmosaics.com

Ravenna Mosaic Co
3126 Nebraska, St Louis, Missouri 63104,
USA

Vedovato Brothers Inc
246 East 116 street, New York, NY 10029,
USA

Australia and New Zealand

Glass Craft Australia
54-56 Lexton Road, Box Hill North,
Victoria, Australia
Tel: (61) 3 9897 4188
Fax: (61) 3 9897 4344

Alan Patrick PTY Ltd
11 Agnes Street, Jolimont, Victoria 3002,
Australia
Tel: (61) 3 9654 8288
Fax: (61) 3 9654 5650

Mosaic Madness
Nola Diamantopoulos
747 (rear) Darling Street
Rozelle
NSW 2039
Australia
Tel: (02) 9818 7471
Email: mailme@mosaicmadness.com.au

Tile Warehouse
Unit 7a, 33 Kaiwharawhara Road,
Wellington, NZ
Tel: (04) 473 9659
Fax: (04) 473 9657

Jacobsen Creative Surfaces
191 Thorndon Quay, Wellington, NZ
Tel: (04) 472 8528
Fax: (04) 472 8530
Email: 4info@jcs.co.nz

Mosaic courses, kits and commissions by Martin Cheek

Martin Cheek runs three-day weekend mosaic courses throughout the year at his and his wife's home in Broadstairs, Kent. He also runs an annual mosaic course every June on the Noel Baker family Candili estate on the island of Evia, Greece. For information about mosaic kits, mosaic materials and mosaic courses please send a large SAE to:
Flint House, 21 Harbour Street, Broadstairs, Kent, CT10 1ET
Website: www.martincheek.com
Email: martin@martincheek.com

This book is dedicated to my dear children, Thomas and Mollie, who are becoming dearer all the time.

Acknowledgements

Over the past few years, I have had to call on the help of talented assistants to get the work made in time, (I'm so slow on my own) and it simply would not have been possible to create the mosaics shown here without what has become a long list of wonderful helpers. Alphabetical order is the only fair way of naming and thanking them all, so here goes: Emma Abel, Kerry Balman, Helen Brooker, Thea Doughty, Laura Elson, Andrew Higgins, Naomi Hope, Rex Hope, Stacey Keeler, Jo Letchford, Laura Plant. I would like to give a special mention to Colette Brannigan, who was my assistant for a long time and was responsible for making many of the beautiful mosaics that are in this book.

The Underwater Panel (see p84) is installed in Guildford, Surrey.
The Leisure Centre Directional Slabs and Activities Mosaic (see p86) are installed in Ramsgate, Kent.

Photograph of *Machynlleth Mela* on pages 38-9 and 61 reproduced by kind permission of Balraj Khanna.

This edition first published in 2003 by
New Holland Publishers (UK) Ltd
London • Cape Town • Sydney • Auckland
www.newhollandpublishers.com

Garfield House
86-88 Edgware Road
London W2 2EA
United Kingdom

80 McKenzie Street
Cape Town 8001
South Africa

14 Aquatic Drive
Frenchs Forest, NSW 2086
Australia

218 Lake Road
Northcote, Auckland
New Zealand

Copyright © 2002 text and designs Martin Cheek
Copyright © 2002 photographs New Holland Publishers (UK) Ltd
Copyright © 2002 New Holland Publishers (UK) Ltd

ISBN 1 84330 141 5

10 9 8 7 6 5 4 3 2

Editor: Kate Haxell
Designer: Roger Hammond
Cover design: Roger Daniels
Photographers: John Freeman and Sean East
Production: Hazel Kirkman
Editorial Direction: Yvonne McFarlane

Reproduction by Modern Age Repro House Ltd., Hong Kong
Printed and bound in Malaysia by Times Offset (M) Sdn. Bhd.

Important
Every effort has been made to present clear and accurate instructions. The author and publishers can accept no liability for injury, illness or damage which may inadvertently be caused to the user while following them.

Index